Enjoying Texts

Also available from Stanley Thornes (Publishers) Ltd:

Learning Me Your Language: Perspectives on the Teaching of English
    edited by Michael Jones and Alastair West
Alternative English: Literature Coursework 16–19
    by C Swatridge

Enjoying Texts

Using Literary Theory in the Classroom

Edited by Mick Burton

Stanley Thornes (Publishers) Ltd

First published in 1989 by:
Stanley Thornes (Publishers) Ltd
Old Station Drive
Leckhampton
CHELTENHAM GL53 0DN
England

British Library Cataloguing in Publication Data
Enjoying texts : using literary theory in the
   classroom.
   1. Literature. Criticism
   I. Burton, M.
   801'.95

   ISBN 1–85234–213–7

Acknowledgement

The publishers would like to express their gratitude for permission to reproduce verses from 'Bogland' by Seamus Heaney, *Door Into The Dark*, Faber and Faber Ltd., p.39.

Typeset by Hunters Armley Ltd., Leeds & London.
Printed and bound in Great Britain at The Bath Press, Avon.

Contents

How to use this book

If you are the sort of reader who likes to start from the beginning and battle your way through to the end, then feel free to do so! If, however, you feel a little tentative about tackling the theories headlong, then browse among the articles, or the first section on English Studies revisited, which places the present situation of English in a brief historical context.

About the articles: they have all been written specially for this volume by practising English teachers. Each is different in scope and style, and in some the theory is more upfront than in others. The most demanding, theoretically, is placed at the end, so by the time you read it you should find the task not too daunting, and, I hope, pleasurable. There should be some spin-off for your own work from many of the articles, subject to age phasing. Perhaps you will have met some of the classroom practices described in the articles before; perhaps you yourself or your colleagues have been engaged in similar work. Good! Where this collection differs from others is in its pointing up, explicitly, of literary theories as a frame from which you can plan work in the classroom. I would also like to imagine that the kinds of work so described and derived will enable children and young adults to become more acute and critical readers and writers.

About the theories section: this is a short and fairly informal guide into a very complex body of knowledge which can seem very indigestible as a lump. So the treatment is often brief, but I hope you will be able to scent the conceptual fragrance at least of the more complex theories. What is most important about reading this section is an open attitude; you probably will find some theories more congenial to your own world view than others. In some cases you may find that not enough space has been given to develop ideas as fully as you would like. However, for each subsection, examples of what the theories might lead to are given, and if they have featured in any of the articles, they will be cross-referenced.

If you decide you wish to read further into any theory, as I hope you do, the bibliography is designed to help, rather than be an academic flourish! Each entry is asterisked according to difficulty, and is briefly annotated. Obviously, theory is a developing academic industry, and ever more books are appearing even as I write this sentence. However, theory does have its own history, and therefore some classic texts of theory have been included. Again, where appropriate, the bibliography is cross-referenced to articles in the book.

The glossary, or harvest of terms, is not meant to be complete, but is intended as a basic set of entries in a dictionary of theoretical terms which could be a good deal longer. However, for each entry, a fairly informal gloss and cross-reference is given, so that you should have at least some idea of what, say, 'deconstruction' is about after looking it up, and whether it is used by any of the contributors.

The main point of reading the book is for you to begin or to continue thinking about the most exciting intellectual developments in the field of English Studies for many years, to talk about them with your colleagues, and to try out for yourselves some of the ideas which you have met in this volume. We are approaching, from official policy, the hardest of times; we need powerful and appropriate counter-measures. Literary theory, used strategically, is such a measure.

1 English Studies revisited

English Studies as a subject in the school and university curriculum has a short history, rich in controversy and dialogue. Out of the radical changes in economic and social formations of the early industrial revolution arose a dissatisfaction with school curricula; the main thrust was towards science and technology, but gradually a focus on English literature developed in the wake of the anxieties of such writers as John Ruskin and Matthew Arnold. In Margaret Mathieson's words, 'Literary men like Ruskin and Matthew Arnold, who disliked the "mechanical" aspects of nineteenth-century England and feared the threat to cultural standards represented by the cheap press, supported the study of literature in desperate tones.'[1] Another critical context for this change was the work of Charles Darwin and Herbert Spencer, which effectively dissolved religious certainty among the rising intellectuals of the later nineteenth century. Spencer asserted that 'Not only, however, for intellectual discipline is science the best; but also for moral discipline.'[2] This emphasis on the positivistic power of science created a space for the nascent subject of English to fill. Its moral significance became inflated to a central position in a liberal education in the thoughts of those for whom religious assurance was a stultifying option.

Matthew Arnold illustrates the situation clearly: '[Culture] seeks to do away with classes; to make the best that has been thought and known in the world current everywhere; to make all men live in an atmosphere of sweetness and light; where they may use ideas, as it uses them itself, freely, nourished, not bound by them . . .'[3] The problem for Arnold is, however, the nature of society as he sees it: 'The mass of mankind will never have any ardent zeal for seeing things as they really are; very inadequate ideas will always satisfy them. On these inadequate ideas reposes, and must repose, the general practice of the world.'[4] Arnold's dilemma is revealing. On the one hand his idea of culture is mythical, removed from the material, historical context; it is universal and free. On the other, he is acutely aware of the alienated condition of 'the mass of mankind' for whom 'things as they really are' are as moribund as their lost religion. It became the territory of English and its teachers, this cultural abyss, and it has been colonized in various ways since. The tradition of Matthew Arnold is inscribed in the work of F.R. Leavis and I.A. Richards in the middle years of this century, and in its turn transformed in their best-known disciple, David Holbrook. Before their ideas are examined further, another strand in the history of English Studies must be unwoven.

In S. Mushet's *Exercises in English* (1912) the following secret code appears:

> 'I had rather go home this way, please.'
> had; Verb. defect. intrans.-act. subj. past indef. sing. 1st-agreeing with "I".
> rather; Advb. of degree, old comparative form-mod. "had"
> go; Verb, strong, intrans.-act. infin. pres.-dep. on "had".'[5]

Before 1920, as Shayer vividly puts it, 'The type of grammar work done in schools was, frankly, nasty.'[6] The concentration on this excessively detailed type of parsing arose from the model of the English used by the textbook writers; English was regarded as an inferior form of Latin. All Mushet's descriptive terms imply a grammar entirely unsuited to modern English.

Not surprisingly, many writers on English teaching began to question the value of such exercises, and began to offer an approach to language work based on the imagination. Typical of such advocates is E. Holmes. In 1911, he attacked the Revised Code, which underscored the Gradgrind approach to grammar, thus: 'as an ingenious instrument for arresting the mental growth of the child, and deadening all his higher faculties, it has never had, and I hope never will have, a rival.'[7] In contrast, Holmes argued for 'the sincere expression in language of the child's genuine thoughts and feelings. The effort to express himself (in language) tends, in proportion as it is sincere and strong, to give breadth, depth and complexity to the child's thoughts and feelings and through the development of these to weave his experiences into the tissue of his life.'[8] A note on the Revised Code of 1861–2 is appropriate here. It was the result of the Newcastle Report of 1851 which noted, among many dubious 'facts', 'a lack of thorough grounding' in the basic subjects. The curriculum was too elaborate, with a goal 'not to make ploughboys or mechanics, but to make scholars'. In each school where 'grants are paid', there should be a 'searching examination of every child, . . . with a view to ascertaining whether these elements of knowledge are thoroughly acquired'.[9] Robert Lowe, the vice-president of the Education Department in 1859, believed that 'the lower classes ought to be educated . . . that they may appreciate and defer to higher motivation.'[10] Accordingly he used the Newcastle Report to justify the creation of his Revised Code. 'We do not profess to give these children an education that will raise them above their station and business in life . . . but to give them an education that may fit them for that business.'[11] The Revised Code now has a rival in its mutant, the National Curriculum.

The emphasis on the individual as creator of meaning did not receive universal blessing, but it is an important stage in the development of English Studies. In 1921, the frequently cited Newbolt Report, *The Teaching of English in England*, thrust aside Classics to proclaim English as the preferred literature in the curriculum; 'no form of literature can take precedence of English literature.'[12] In thus signalling the change of focus, the Report also attempted to resolve Arnold's dilemma; good English teaching would be 'the greatest benefit which could be conferred on any citizen . . . and the common right to it, the common discipline and enjoyment of it, the common possession of the tastes and associations connected with it, would form a new element of national unity, linking together the mental life of all classes . . .'[13]

These powerful and far-reaching claims for the centrality of English literature in Newbolt received radical underpinning in the work of F.R. Leavis and his followers at Cambridge in the thirties and forties. The influence of Leavis, together with that of I.A. Richards, has been pervasive throughout the practices of English teaching particularly since the late fifties. In Leavis's lofty prose, English 'trains, in a way no other discipline can, intelligence and sensitivity together, cultivating a sensitiveness and precision of response, and a delicate integrity of intelligence that integrates as well as analyses, and must have pertinacity as well as delicacy.'[14] I shall unpack the complexities of this intellectual baggage later; for the moment we may turn to Richards: 'The world of poetry has in no sense any different reality from the rest of the world and it has no special laws and no other-worldly peculiarities. It is made up of experiences of exactly the same kinds as those that come to us in other ways . . . it is more highly and delicately organised than ordinary experiences.'[15] Embedded in the first sentence is an amazingly naive view of the relationship between language and reality. As his other writings show, Richards imagined language to be transparent, to offer a plate-glass view of other minds and of the real world. Hence it was in principle possible to cultivate the minds of readers to the right perspectives on life through reading good literature. This was an imperative task, as 'At present bad literature, bad art, the cinema, etc., are an influence of the first importance in fixing immature and actually inapplicable attitudes to most things.'[16] Richards' main legacy for the teaching of English stems from his notion of practical criticism, that close reading of words on the page which closes when the reader recreates in the process of reading 'the relevant experience of the poet when contemplating the completed composition.'[17] This seemingly harmless objective has in practice led to a textual authoritarianism under which generations of school-children have been dragooned into believing that there can be only one response to a text, and that if they do not show it, they are barbarians.

In many ways the influences of Leavis and Richards are crystallized in the work of David Holbrook. He takes their concerns and claims as frames of reference, while concentrating, in strategic terms, on the development of the pupil as an individual through creative expression and response. His approach is well summed up in the address he gave to the Dartmouth Seminar.[18] He claims that 'Effective English teaching, in that it has to do with the whole complex of language in our lives, has to do with the whole problem of the individual identity and how it develops.'[19] Holbrook was very aware of the work of the psychoanalyst Melanie Klein, who argued that our adult identity derives from a very early splitting of the infant self, which is filled with anxiety and turmoil. She writes,

> The repeated attempts that have been made to improve humanity – in particular to make it more peaceable – have failed, because nobody has understood the full depth and vigour of the instincts of aggression innate in each individual . . . the resolution of early infantile anxiety not only lessens and modifies the child's aggressive impulses, but leads to a more valuable employment of them from a social point of view.[20]

Holbrook's publications, such as *English for Maturity* and *English for the Rejected*, offered an exciting and liberating approach to teachers of English in the sixties. I certainly began my teaching career from a point of view structured by Holbrook's ideas, for he emphasized the worth of the individual pupil, regardless of his or her ability. Yet at the back of his concerns was the élitist concept of culture he had inherited from Leavis, which also became articulated in the work of Denys Thompson. The flavour of Thompson's menu for English is given in a book he wrote with Leavis in 1942, *Culture and Environment*: 'We cannot, as we might in a healthy state of culture, leave the citizen to be formed unconsciously by his environment; if anything like a worthy idea of satisfactory living is to be saved, he must be trained to discriminate and resist.'[21]

While this concern for the individual was orientated towards literature, official worry about working-class underachievement became public with the Newsom Report of 1963, *Half Our Future*. It identified linguistic competence as the key factor in educational success, although not in the terms of the rampant parsiphiles of the beginning of the century. From this initial step emerged various research programmes in the field of language and education. The best-known educational material developed by the programmes was *Language in Use* and *Breakthrough to Literacy*. The most problematic outcome of the research was Basil Bernstein's *Class, Codes and Control*, especially volume 1. In practical terms, it appeared that language use differed radically between working-class and middle-class speakers. The 'language of the school' was biased towards middle-class children, and working-class children couldn't use it, except by an enormous effort of code-switching, to what was dubbed 'elaborated code'. There followed a fierce debate, not helped by simplistic transmissions of early Bernstein as revealed truth by keen lecturers in Colleges of Education. At issue are the felt differences between working-class and middle-class cultures and the way these cultures are given linguistic articulation. Subsequent research, especially that of Gordon Wells,[22] showed that the differences were not neatly arranged across class groupings; however, the fundamental differences of culture remain, as significant issues for the English teacher, especially with the publication, in April 1988, of the Kingman Report. Some of the ground covered by my mention of the ghastly grammar books of the early twentieth century is now, with this report, exhumed. I shall consider it later, in chapter 10.

Two further influences on the development of English teaching need mention here. The National Association for the Teaching of English was inaugurated in 1963, and was originally run by followers of Leavis such as Boris Ford and Frank Whitehead. It has since, through conferences, and especially its journal, *English in Education*, been a powerful focus for new directions in English teaching. As yet, with the vibrant exception of the Language and Gender group, NATE has not been identified with literary theories and their place in mainstream English teaching. Its journal accurately reflects the plurality, eccentricity and interests of a wide range of practices. It is a complex mirror of precisely those uncertainties about English as a subject which have rendered it so open to attack in the present climate of education. Yet it is an absolutely serious focus for dialogue. The Spring 1988 issue, for example, is an excellent, wide-ranging problematizing of the notion of oracy, with an incisive critique of the Assessment of Performance Unit's work in this field; 'the APU seem to be totally unaware of issues of language diversity relating to social and cultural background.'[23]

Since the early sixties, the work of James Britton, Nancy Martin and Harold Rosen has been in the foreground of developments in English teaching. To list some of their publications outlines their main concerns: *Language and Learning, Language, the Learner and the School, Writing and Learning across the Curriculum, The Development of Writing Abilities 11–18, The Language and Dialects of London Schoolchildren*, have been formative of many liberating practices. Tony Burgess summarizes their framing influence thus: '. . . it is because human beings live in history that they have need of language; . . . if human beings never had to cope with change, which they could not control or predict, they would not need language as their cure or care in the perils and possibilities of living.'[24] For the writers from the London Institute of Education, language is the key focus. But since the model of language built up from many sources is dialogical, assuming that the pupil brings a valid system to school, it allows for much more open practices in the classroom. Talking and writing are seen as modes of learning, of exploratory activity, not merely reproductions of Culture. Reading is of a wide variety of texts, including media. Listening is part of the collaborative making of meanings that a dialogic model of language implies. From this perspective literature is not thrown out of the classroom, but its parameters are widened. It is no longer the Great White Canon – a selective tradition of texts written by men – but much more catholic. The contrast with Leavis and his followers is striking. I must point out, however, that this short summary conceals a wide range of differences – Britton and Rosen did not share the same views of language and society, for instance.

The theories I have cited above are all in some way formative of English practice in the late eighties. To call them theories is perhaps puzzling at first sight. Leavis, for example, strenuously denied, in an exchange with Wellek, that theory was anything to do with criticism.[25] However, as Halliday reminds us, anyone who uses language has a theory.[26] Not necessarily a scientifically organized body of concepts, but a way of seeing, of understanding the world, which constitutes our very experience. In simple terms, we cannot help being positioned by language. We always have a viewpoint. For Leavis, however, and his followers, the goal of their discourse was to deny any partiality; to naturalize, and thus make appear inevitable, what they said about literary texts. So their position seemed unassailable, since it claimed not to be a position at all. The text would reflect back the finest feelings of a discriminating sensibility beamed on it, in sheer transparency: 'This – doesn't it? – bears such a relation to that; this kind of thing – don't you find it so? – wears better than that.'[27] What if one says 'No'?

The Leavisite language games employed a set of terms designed to reinforce this overall strategy. Terry Eagleton lists some of these: 'sensitive, imaginative, responsive, sympathetic, creative, perceptive, reflective. Notice the resounding intransitivity of all these familiar shibboleths.'[28] Being intransitive, that is, not acting upon anything in particular, these terms seem to be absolutes, or universals; about everything. This is an empty position; cultural signs are historically specific and to attempt to embalm them in eternal Truth is the act of a cultural patriarch. A clear example of this process is Cleanth Brooks' analysis of Keats' 'Ode on a Grecian Urn'. Brooks takes as central the paradox of the stone narrating truths about life; the urn has a voice and enunciates eternal truths about human transience, but it is inanimate. Brooks' analysis halts at the paradox; for all the New Critics, 'Poems remain, and explain.'[29] How, I wonder, would a reader approach the text today? What images of Greece, ancient or modern, are now available? The corrupt colonels democratizing torture? Melina Mercouri requesting the UK government to return the so-called Elgin Marbles? Swarming yuppies staining white rock? How does a woman read 'Thou still unravished bride of quietness'?

English Studies as it is in the late eighties has developed from many pressure points and different sources. I have mentioned two pathways in particular: one, the cultural heritage, stems from Matthew Arnold via Leavis and his followers; the other, the language-as-baseline approach, stems from grinding a bastardized Latin grammar into English words, and becomes radically transformed through the various perspectives of progressive and language-centred practices. At the time of writing this introduction, there is another pressure point which the contributors to the book have acknowledged and transformed into strategies of classroom practice: literary theory. At one level, namely that of university studies, literary theory has been incorporated into degree structures over the last fifteen years as an essential component of the study of literature, as well as media and film. As yet, its application to English Studies in the classroom is not widespread, but there is a considerable body of practice which uses insights from theories of literature as a framework for planning classroom activities. The articles that follow show how, far from being locked in some esoteric academic realm of discourse, literary theories are a very useful base from which to devise English teaching which opens more texts than it closes.

NOTES

1 Margaret Mathieson, *The Preachers of Culture*, London, George Allen and Unwin Ltd, 1975, p.26.

2 Sir Herbert Spencer, 'Science and Religion', in A. Low Beer,ed., *Spencer*, London, Collier-Macmillan, 1969, p.55.

3 Matthew Arnold, *Culture and Anarchy*, Ann Arbor, University of Michigan Press, 1965, p.112.

4 Matthew Arnold, 'Equality', in *Mixed Essays: The Works of Matthew Arnold*, London, Edition de Luxe, 1903, p.91.

5 Mushet, *Exercises in English*, 1912, cited in Shayer, *The Teaching of English* (see n.6) pp. 20–1.

6 David Shayer, *The Teaching of English in Schools 1900–1970*, London, Routledge and Kegan Paul, 1972, p.20.

7 E. Holmes, *What Is and What Might Be*, London, Constable, 1911, cited in Shayer, *The Teaching of English*, p.39.

8 Holmes, *What Is and What Might Be*, cited in Mathieson, *The Preachers of Culture*, p.61.

9 Christopher Martin, *A Short History of English Schools*, Hove, Wayland Publishers Ltd, 1979, p.18.

10 ibid., pp.18–19.

11 ibid., p.19.

12 *The Teaching of English in England*, London, HMSO, 1921, p.14.

13 ibid., p.15.

14 F.R. Leavis, *Education and the University*, London, Chatto and Windus, 1943, p.34.

15 I.A. Richards, *Principles of Literary Criticism*, London, Routledge and Kegan Paul, 1966, p.78.

16 ibid., pp.202–3.

17 ibid., p.178.

18 The Dartmouth Seminar was a key conference of Anglo-American English teachers held in 1966 to address the perceived crisis in the teaching of English. See David Allen, *English Teaching Since 1965: How Much Growth?*, London, Heinemann, 1980, chapters 1–3.

19 David Holbrook, 'Remarks to the Dartmouth Seminar', in Allen, *English Teaching Since 1965*, p.21.

20 J.A.C. Brown, *Freud and the Post-Freudians*, Harmondsworth, Penguin, 1961, p.76.

21 Mathieson, *The Preachers of Culture*, p.122.

22 Gordon Wells, *Language Learning and Education*, London, NFER – Nelson, 1985.

23 Janet Maybin, 'A critical review of the DES Assessment of Performance Unit's Oracy Survey', NATE *English in Education*, Spring 1988.

24 Tony Burgess, 'The Question of English', in Margaret Meek and Jane Miller, eds., *Changing English: Essays for Harold Rosen*, London, Heinemann, 1984, p.2.

25 Ann Jefferson and David Robey, eds., *Modern Literary Theory: A Comparative Introduction*, London, Batsford, 1986, pp.5–6.

26 Michael Halliday, 'Linguistic Function and Literary Style: an inquiry into the language of William Golding's *The Inheritors*', part reprinted in Mary Douglas, ed., *Rules and Meanings*, Harmondsworth, Penguin, 1973.

27 Jefferson and Robey, *Modern Literary Theory*, pp.5–6.

28 Terry Eagleton, 'The Bankruptcy of Liberal Human Values in Literary Studies', *ILEA English Magazine* 15.

29 William Wimsatt and Monroe Beardsley, 'The Affective Fallacy', reprinted in David Lodge, ed., *20th Century Literary Criticism: A Reader*, London, Longman, 1972, p.357.

2 Enabling readers to open up texts
Tess Collingborn

Tess Collingborn has taught in Tanzania, Manchester, Crawley and Swindon, where she is currently second in the English department at Dorcan School. She has been an advisory teacher, and has conducted research into writing for GCSE. She is assistant chief moderator for GCSE English Literature for the Northern Examining Association. She took her M.Ed. at Bristol University, where she became particularly interested in the relations between literary theory, autobiography and the attempt to establish or construct an identity. She now seeks to inform her own teaching with these insights.

When introducing a new class-reader, a useful preliminary, with pupils of all ages, is to focus attention on the book itself as an object or artefact. This can be done by asking pupils what the front cover suggests to them. Here the title and accompanying illustration are the basis for a prediction exercise which involves the pupil-reader in consideration of content, genre and focus – what the story is about, what kind of story it is likely to be, who or what is the main character, what kind of person she/he may be, why the particular illustration was chosen. A short burst of writing, prior to discussion, enables each pupil to jot down her/his thoughts and responses.

Normally when we begin reading, we immerse ourselves in the story, after a cursory glance at cover and title. The prediction exercise described above also begins to involve the reader with the story, but in a way that is less passive and surrendering, and which highlights and extends the questioning and deciding process involved in the cursory glance. Looking *at* the book and considering its exterior before 'getting into' it is an activity that simultaneously involves the reader with and distances her from the text, enabling her to view the book as an object that has been put together, a construct or artefact about which choices and decisions have been made. This serves to reduce the authority of 'the book' as simply there and as it is. It empowers the reader by suggesting her ability to make comment on and decisions about the book. It also reduces the power of the author as privileged and omniscient about writing.

Seeing the book as an object whose elements have been chosen by other human agents implies that its constitutive parts may be questioned, challenged, and – ultimately – changed. The pupil is asserted as an agent in relation to the book as product, as a self who is operating as a mediator of the meaning of the text.

This challenging is not something secondary-school pupils, by and large, are used to doing with the objects or circumstances of their lives. Sadly, they are too often presented with packaged goods, whether toys, foods or experiences, transformer-robot, Action Man, Barbie doll, My Little Pony or the 'spectacle' and 'experience' of certain museums or 'theme-parks'. The toy or food or experience inevitably bears, in its packaging and presentation, a great weight of cultural assumptions. The stiff, blonde Barbie doll with an endless wardrobe presents to little girls the culturally acceptable shape of womanhood – slim, glamorous, to be put in a limited range of poses, to be manipulated; while the transformer-robot presents to boys the manipulative, transforming, technologically orientated and essentially destructive image of Rambo-manhood. The analysis could be extended into teenage and special interest magazines. But the point is sufficiently clear that pupils should be encouraged to question, in order to understand, the many and various cultural artefacts with which they are presented and which shape their attitudes and ideas.

The interrogation of the book-cover, with its simultaneous involvement and distancing, constitutes a more honest, open and accessible approach for the majority of pupils than the traditional literary criticism. The latter is a highly sophisticated mode of operation which, even while encouraging the 'personal response', still enshrines an accepted canon of literary works, of tastes, and even of responses. Rather than seeing books and writing as something produced in, and in response to, the culture of their times, the traditional Leavis/Richards approach embodies a powerful idea of universality and continuity, of unchanging ideals and certainties. Such an approach can seem to ignore and hence to devalue our contemporary uncertainties, and quests, in response to different forces and conditions.

By drawing pupils' attention to books as artefacts, one is highlighting for them their scope as individual agents, their scope to exercise their own judgements, while also pointing up the existence of structures and institutions – publishing companies, editors, designers – which have purposes and priorities of their own, and which aim to influence or even manipulate – a highly charged word – the choices of readers. Of course, such notions may well not be presented to pupils overtly, especially to younger pupils; yet the presentation of book-as-artefact does still imply these ideas even when they are not spelled out. This touches on the way in which we all partake of the public sphere, our experience, thoughts, opinions and memories all being shaped and mediated by the public – public events, attitudes and means of communication – as well as by what is domestic, intimate and personal.

Encouraging pupils to see themselves as questioners of and commentators upon the book can also serve to make them more critical as readers, and more aware of themselves as interpreters and shapers of the meaning of the text. Thus the record of their first impressions of and predictions about the book/ story can be supplemented and compared with later responses to a prediction about the story, both at particular moments and at the end. This can be done simply on two or three occasions, or as a more detailed 'reading log' monitoring the varying and extending understanding, misunderstanding and questioning of character, event, theme and plot.

This focus on the reader's developing responses, and thus on the way in which she mediates and makes the text, is part way towards foregrounding the Lacanian idea of the split subject, the distinction or gap between the grammatical subject and the speaker, or, as Roman Jakobson puts it, between the 'enounced', that is, narrated event and the 'enunciation', that is, the act of utterance. In the above example the text or story is the 'enounced', while the pupil/reader is the one who utters what is announced, that is, the one who produces meaning.

One can put it another way and use Saussure's terms. The printed book is the signifier and the story that it recounts is the signified. These two together constitute the 'sign', that is, the storybook, to which the reader gives meaning. Yet, for Lacan, meaning is endlessly deferred: the attainment of the fullness of meaning is illusory. Thus the way is open for a multiplicity of meanings, of incomplete and constantly revised interpretations. And isn't this what we are involved in when reading or re-reading a story, play or poem?

Having read the chosen text with a class, there are a variety of ways in which one can encourage pupils to make meaning from it. Thus an invitation to 'pick out' words, phrases/sentences from Samuel Beckett's play *Endgame* and insert them into a poem produced the following from a fifth-year pupil:

> Nothing stirs, all is ZERO!
> Like black – from pole to pole.
> There's no one else.
> There's nowhere else.
> It's time it ended.
>
> Gone from me you'd be dead.
> Outside of here it's death.
> Let's stop playing,
> Put me in my coffin.
> Then let it end! With a bang!
> Of DARKNESS!

Undeniably, the poem works in its own right, having a shape and meaning of its own. At the same time it conveys clearly and strongly the bleakness of Beckett's vision as presented in the play, particularly from the viewpoint of Hamm. The writer has involved herself thoughtfully with the text and presented a particular version and convincing vision of her own. To denigrate this poem as merely 'copying' would be to ignore the thinking and the shaping of language that has been involved in reading and understanding the play, in selecting and organizing the lines of the poem. The acknowledgement of this poem underlines M.M. Bakhtin's assertion that 'the word in language is half someone else's.' It highlights the way in which we all use other people's words that we have heard in other contexts – an honourable tradition, sanctioned by Eliot in 'The Waste Land': 'These fragments I have shored against my ruins.' Words always come to us freighted with the meanings which others have given them, and our use of them adds yet other subtle variations. To quote Bakhtin again: 'There are no "neutral" words and forms . . . Language . . . is populated – overpopulated – with the intentions of others.' Multiple meanings held in simultaneity thus are ever-present, even if overlooked or ignored.

A way of drawing pupils' attention to multiple meanings or alternative interpretations is to ask them what scenes are 'missing' from a play and to write them themselves. In this, one is laying bare concealed assumptions, and locating and foregrounding the 'absent signifiers' – that which has been left out but which, by its very absence, contributes to the meaning of the text. This way of interrogating the text both focuses on its overt meaning and also subverts it. It necessitates a to-and-fro movement between the text as 'given' by the author and the text produced by the pupil.

The play *The Widowing of Mrs Holroyd* by D.H. Lawrence can be fruitfully approached in this manner. The play was read with a mixed-ability group of fifth-year pupils. At various points during the reading, the pupils were asked to adopt the role of one of the three main characters, Mrs Holroyd, Holroyd, or Blackmore, and to write that person's account of and comment on what was happening. This could be the basis of a more extended piece written in character. It also led on to a discussion of what differences there would be in the play if the focus was on Holroyd rather than on his wife. What scenes could be added? What would be said about Mrs Holroyd? About Blackmore?

Pupils were then set a variety of 'missing scenes' to write:
- Holroyd in the pub with the two 'trollops', Clara and Laura;
- Clara and Laura, on the way home, discuss their encounter with Holroyd and his wife;
- the elder Mrs Holroyd discusses her son and daughter-in-law with her husband or a neighbour.

A further document could be the newspaper account of the pit accident in which Holroyd dies.

These tasks allow for a variety of styles of writing, since pupils can present them as a story or a play or news article. They also allow pupils to write at whatever length their understanding or interest dictates. This alleviates the burden of those who feel unable to sustain a simple, lengthy, 'objective', essay-type piece of writing, the several shorter pieces giving opportunity for different aspects and moments of the text to be approached separately. Such 'imaginative responses' can and do demonstrate a close, lively and detailed understanding of the play. To write convincingly about Holroyd, his mother or the 'paper bonnets', the pupil must show that 'understanding of and involvement in' the text which GCSE syllabuses require: an awareness of character, action and motivation. Yet even if the pupil's writing does not fit closely to such criteria, it is still valid as a piece of writing in itself (assuming each piece has some coherence of its own) and as an expression of the pupil's own ideas informed by the reading of the play.

Another text, one that is perhaps more familiar to teachers of fourth-and fifth-year pupils, and which can be approached through locating its shifts and gaps, is Brighouse's *Hobson's Choice*. The activities described are best done in small groups. At an early point in the reading of the play, I asked pupils to write a list ranking the characters according to strength of personality. At the end of the play, a revised rank order was written and the changes discussed. Obviously this draws out the ways in which characters have developed and relationships have altered.

They were also asked which character they would trust most and which they would prefer as a friend. These two questions did not always elicit the same response, and the reasons given can throw up interesting or important points about trust and friendship, as well as about the particular characters and their actions.

Another activity involved the pupils, in pairs, plotting three lines on a graph to show where the three main characters, Maggie, Willie Mossop and Hobson, stand in relation to each other at the start of the play and where they are situated at the end of the play. To explain the graph, they also had to indicate what happened and when in order to alter the direction of the lines of the graph. This graph makes visually very plain the varying relationship of the three characters, focusing attention on where power and authority lie, who is or is not powerful, when and how their power is exercised, and, indeed, what constitutes power or strength. Pupils are actively involved in lively argument, making decisions about what they think has happened in the play and what is the meaning of the events.

One can go even further and present pupils with a self-consciously reflective text, the kind which undercuts itself by drawing attention to itself as a fictional construct rather than purporting to be a transparent 'window on the world'. Such a play is Beckett's *Endgame* in which, at various points, the characters refer to their essentially repetitive and consciously constructed game-like situation, for instance 'Me to play.' I have used this text successfully with a mixed-ability fifth-year group. Notwithstanding the initial response, 'This isn't a proper play' (what assumptions were they working on?), we had several lively, thoughtful and fruitful discussions, not least about the game-like aspects of the play – the ways in which it imitates essential elements of other games, whether team games, such as football, or boardgames. The parallel with chess was obviously canvassed, and one pupil, not among the most able in the class, commented on the way in which people in 'real' life are ranked according to ability or disability, cleverness or stupidity, akin to the way teams are ranked in a football league.

Endgame is a text whose content, discourse and structure are remote from today's secondary pupils and to which they do not readily or easily gain access. Writing about such a text can present difficulties, but here decentring or distruptive strategies are particularly useful. Rewriting the ending of the play, writing a further scene, or an earlier scene which explores how the characters come to be where they are at the start of the play – all of these allow for imaginative extensions of the play, enabling many pupils to get to closer grips with the text than does a 'straightforward' essay. Such writing allows for freer play of the individual's attempt to make meaning, to interrogate and interpret the text in the light of her own understanding and experience. Thus the pupil makes the text her own, making sense of it and retelling it in her own way.

Working along these lines, one pupil produced a 'prior scene' of the play in which the power-relationship between Clov and Hamm was reversed. Other such scenes presented street-gang or Mafia-type conflicts to explain the disabilities and restricted movement of Beckett's characters. One pupil, exploring further scenes to the play, sent Clov out into the world, and then brought him back to the womb-like safety of Beckett's bleak room with a repetition of Beckett's own words at the start of his play.

Writing in these ways allows pupils to demonstrate their understanding of the text that has been read and to construct their own interpretation and response, often capturing the style of the author's language, and thus writing in a mode they would otherwise have been unaware of and not attempted.

Another way of opening up a text for readers is the use of spider charts to focus on what a character is and does. This proved particularly helpful as a way into the character of Mr Crouch in T.F. Powys's short story 'Lie Thee Down, Oddity!' Pupils found this deceptively simple story difficult to get to grips with, saying it was 'rubbish, boring, stupid'. Yet when asked to note on a spider chart what Mr Crouch is and does, their understanding was demonstrably greater than they themselves had perceived. Being asked thus to deal with the straightforward matter of the story, their own group discussion led them gently to consider its much more difficult meaning.

An even more disruptive strategy is to ask pupils to present an alternative version of a text. Such activities can be done with a play like Bill Owen's *The Laundry Girls*. All the characters are girls and the setting is a turn-of-the-century laundry. What happens when the characters are turned into boys? When the setting – both physical and historical – is changed? The topics of conversation changed? Each of these changes involves the pupils in interrogating the text and taking power to create their own texts.

All of the above activities have been used with mixed-ability groups in a comprehensive school. All of them have led to pupils involving themselves with often demanding texts, and all have resulted in each pupil, individually and collaboratively, making sense of the texts and making them their own.

3 GCSE post-structuralism: it can be done!

Nick Peim

Nick Peim has been a comprehensive-school English teacher for twelve years and is currently Head of English and Drama at Beauchamp College, a large Leicestershire upper school and community college. He is also an advanced postgraduate student at Leicester University, attempting to investigate aspects of the changing discourses of English. He is especially interested in psychoanalysis and its effects on the theory of culture, as well as the theories of Michel Foucault and the politics of English.

Why should English teachers at this particular juncture of the history of English in schools bother with literary theory? There is, after all, a lot to be said against it. The language of literary theory is often peculiarly complicated, can be sometimes deliberately obscure – and is very remote from the languages of the people we teach. It's élitist, exclusive, academic; it promotes a star system of intellectual superheroes and an ever-lengthening cast of supporting acolytes. It inhabits the 'academy' – a world very much removed from the hard realities of comprehensive schools. It is contemptuous of common sense, has little time for experience, refuses to have truck with simplicity and directness. It's brutal: it attacks our most cherished assumptions about the value of what we teach, destabilizes our central ideas, our established practices, and calls many productive activities into question.

Remote, chic, avant-garde, intellectually haughty, pointlessly inaccessible and generally too unwieldy to furnish practical ideas for teaching, literary theory has discussed its rewritings of English literature with scant reference to English teaching in schools. As academic literary theory – intoxicated with its own intellectual achievements – spirals dizzyingly into ever more circular debates about post-modernism, post-colonialism, post-capitalism, it seems to leave the realities of the mass medium of English teaching in schools far behind.

At the same time, aspects of theory represent immense power of ideas. Structuralism and post-structuralism constitute a massive field encompassing quite revolutionary ways of understanding fundamental issues and questions about the whole field of cultural practices, including everything that has ever come under the heading of English literature, whatever the brand of the discourse. The major productions – in terms of ideas – of theory, whether in the field of psychoanalysis or literary studies, can promote a whole new way of thinking about language, representation and communication. These are, potentially, immensely productive in the way they address cultural objects and practices.

Literary theory is to do with much more than literature or with theories about literature alone, calling into question the privileges granted to the category 'literature' and the processes of exclusion that its maintenance often involves. Literary theory begins with ideas about what literature is, then addresses itself to the whole field of cultural production and reception, and examines the wider social context within which these things are constructed. Thus it can change the 'object' of study, alter practice and extend the field of view of the subject, drawing into itself thought from other discourses that may have a bearing on this newly defined field of knowledge.

One name for this field could be GCSE English and English Literature.

All language is sign language

In spite of the mystique of literary theory, teaching aspects of semiotics with fourth- and fifth-year classes is perfectly possible without making reference to any prohibitively difficult ideas. 'Theoretical' terminology can be usefully introduced, can be illustrated, and can be handed over, as it were, simply and directly. Once in the hands of students, activities and working structures can be developed which will engage them in a more active appropriation and utilization of theory. The first and fundamental terms of semiotics, for example, establishing the analysis of the sign as composed of signifier and signified – soon to become the objects of much 'play' in a more general drive towards deconstruction – can be quickly illustrated and can then immediately lead to some 'practical' applications.

A class of fourth-years, newly arrived into the 14–18 community college, with varying levels of ability ascribed to them by the high schools they've just left, embarking on the course that will take them, via the certification machinery, to GCSE English and English Literature, are invited to give examples of signs – any kind of signs: traffic lights, road signs, written signs, picture signs, signs on toilet doors. A discussion can then follow about how the signs work. The terms 'signifier' and 'signified' can be introduced and explained, according to the simple Saussurian definition of the structure of the sign. The traffic lights example provides a useful model for discussing the idea of a sign system in relation to a specific cultural practice: the traffic lights constitute a discrete (Saussurian) sign system, but one which operates within the cultural practice (discourse) of road-use and which is related to other signs and other sign systems (discourses). The arbitrary nature of the sign – how the signifier relates to the signified in no intrinsic way – may also, though it represents a very significant theoretical leap, be discussed quite simply. This major and potentially radically deconstructive point – sometimes alluded to in mysterious terms as the free-floating signifier – in this context can be used to exemplify the way that contexts and conventions, rather than meanings, give signs particular values and directions. A couple of fifty-minute lessons would be enough to convey all this. From such a starting point, activities can be devised and offered to make the ideas more properly available for exploration, discussion and debate.

From the humble example of the traffic lights and the perhaps not so humble toilet door, introducing the ideologically loaded issue of gender, the analysis of signs in language can follow. (That is, language language as opposed to traffic lights language or some other kind of sign language.) The example can be taken of a single, fairly simple – written and spoken – signifier, 'dog': what is the signified? The response is likely to be varied. A list of different signifieds can be compiled by the whole class to illustrate how the signified is not held in any simple, single relationship to the signifier. Equally important, the signified also turns out, in this case, to be at one time one thing, at another something different, but on the way it has been set up, finally, to be an indefinitely long list of other signifiers; though not necessarily, perhaps hardly ever, all of these at once. The implications of these points – which do not seem to be entirely consonant with familiar and with common-sense notions of language – can be further teased out by examining other kinds of signifiers in language: conjunctions, shifters, adjectives, and so on. Important ideas, fundamental to structuralist and post-structuralist thinking have been dealt with here: the predominance of the (free-floating) signifier, the deferral of meaning and the signifying chain, the cultural specificity of discourses or language-games, for instance: all of which can be (and often are) described in arcane terminology with knotty syntax, but which don't have to be.

The preparatory stage need not take long nor be over-complicated. The problematic nature of the sign in language has been established. Semiotic thinking and analysis is under way; common sense has been displaced; English lessons are not quite what they used to be. The use of signs within different kinds of sign systems and the relationship between signs, sign systems and cultural practices has, in a preliminary way, been illustrated. Students, who at this stage are unlikely to have formulated any explicit models of the workings of language, are quick to take up these points and can make them their own with relative ease. The conceptual matter they're dealing with is, after all, no more difficult than, say, topics in geometry. The vocabulary is no more alienating than some they'll come across in design subjects. It isn't necessary to assume that semiotics (nor deconstruction, theory of discourses and related concerns), because it has become associated with the 'high' and exclusive (excluding) culture of academic discourse, is therefore inaccessible to fourteen- and fifteen-year-olds. To assume necessarily that it is may well be to discredit their capacities as well as to collude with the academic inflection of these ideas, and of ideas in general.

Introducing cultural practices

The theoretical apparatus has been established: some practical exploration can now take place. The exercise to begin with is to take two common signifiers and produce lists, individually or in pairs or in small groups, of 'signifieds' for the culturally loaded terms 'man' and 'woman'. Two separate lists are to be written on either side of a page divided lengthwise into two. Games may then follow, including pairing terms, finding what terms can't readily be paired, grouping terms to do with activities, listing clothing, grouping adjectives and then, perhaps, analysing through discussion the implications of these findings. Important points about the cultural power of signifiers can emerge from these kinds of discussions. The gender issue is one which is not particularly unfamiliar and so the proposed new terminology and new way of examining language should be unhindered. As gender divisions are so much actively constructed and reproduced through everyday linguistic exchange, students will find themselves quickly making their own discoveries.

Two particularly useful terms in this context, which can be stored for further use, development and reference, are metaphor and metonymy – according to Lacan's use of Jakobson, the twin axes of language. The man and woman lists are likely to throw into sharp relief many examples of metonym and metaphor which can make some explicit pointing of their effects. Their importance relates closely to what has already been hinted at in the arbitrary structure of the sign, as the ever-shifting chain of signification, the elusive trail of fixed meaning. The ways in which they displace and defer meaning can be illustrated by the students themselves using their own examples. Very attractive, amusing and powerfully illustrative displays can be mounted using pictorial representations of metonyms and metaphors that students have produced.

At any stage in the progress of the work being described here, students can be told that what they are studying is semiotics relating to cultural practices, that they are learning about or actually actively conducting an examination of signs at work in specific cultural practices; that they are developing an understanding of language (in relation to the construction of social meanings and social realities) that doesn't always accord with common sense, but that is nonetheless perfectly sensible, demonstrable and useful in terms of practical analyses and which is theoretically more powerful and inclusive than common sense. The practical analysis can then become the point at which the students themselves take control of their work. They are invited to consider examples of representations/constructions of gender distinctions using signs in children's fictions, magazines (of any kind), television adverts and soap operas. Before or during this stage it can be useful to spend more time discussing cultural practices – what kinds of things they are, how they work, in what contexts, to what effects – in a general and open-ended kind of way. Students select their own examples, their own texts, to emphasize that to begin with we're interested in any manifestations of the form or genre in question, that representations of gender differences are likely to be pervasively present in cultural practices concerned with common social life.

Some time is spent with students in class examining in detail their own selections of magazines, children's stories, television soap operas and adverts, time to draw up lists of examples of various kinds of representations of gender in these media. It's an important element of this kind of work, I think, to allow students to work on these tasks collaboratively with the teacher available for clarification, especially as new ideas and terminology are being introduced. All of this phase, where students are collecting examples, attempting to analyse how they work and what their likely effects are, may be prefaced by whole-group activities which examine initial instances together. With one fourth-year group we've discussed a single *Peter and Jane* text collectively, and done collectively a kind of semiotic analysis of the Swan kitchen magazine advert and the Pretty Polly tights poster advert, paying particular attention to metonymic evocations of femininity, ultimately asking whether these evocations are not, in fact, products or constructions more than neutral representations of ideals. With the right kind of clarity in the questioning and openness in response, ensuring that students are always given time to formulate their own responses first and ensuring that most of the discussion comes from them, detailed and quite sophisticated analyses are possible.

The final result of all this work could well be a piece for GCSE examination coursework, and could equally be submitted for the English or the English Literature folder. It is important, as I've said, that students work collaboratively – and that they do so consciously. Any kind of cultural studies project that fails to emphasize that aspect of the work fails, I think, to grasp some essential points about the kind of classroom organization that is most desirable, but equally is most likely to give rise to questions about common assumptions, popular myths, individual differences and ways that all these often conflicting factors are involved in the reception of cultural signs and in the production of sign systems. The specifications of the GCSE criteria demand, for obvious and highly deconstructable reasons, that all pieces submitted should be the individual work of the candidates. That doesn't, though, discount students working closely on the organization, detail and handling of ideas in one another's writings. An 'essay' can be produced which is the individual product of an individual student yet which has been produced in close dialogue with others who may have commented on its contents, argued its ideas through, suggested developments in the analyses it enacts and the form it finally takes. This way of encouraging students to work counteracts the absurdly limited model of language which grants true authenticity only to the individual consciousness, and it inexplicitly affirms the notion that cultural phenomena can only be properly understood collectively.

This example – of teaching about cultural practices in relation to gender constructions through an understanding of how signs work – is one chosen from many possible examples, and is intended to illustrate how semiotics, or some of its terms and ideas, can be put to use in an introductory way with incoming fourth-year students. Since the schemes we teach at GCSE are of the Mode 3 persuasion, there's absolutely no problem about any of the content of course-work pieces being disallowed or subject to negative scrutiny by external controlling examiners who may have different ideas about what is and isn't legitimately English. This open freedom means that the kind of work already described can be conceived as preliminary to an indefinite number of other related activities that raise issues of textual and extra-textual relations, which will begin from some of the themes announced in the phase of work described above. What follows is not at all offered as the outline of a course that follows progressively through a necessary continuum of themes or topics. I have rather attempted to describe examples of discrete activities which may follow different directions from those I've suggested and which may be variously related to one another. There will always be significant connections between the particular topics described, and these strands can be made more or less explicit.

From semiotics to deconstruction: textual analysis

A general deconstruction of some of the privileged categories of English can begin at almost any point and can involve any activity concerned with the de-centring of any text, set of texts, reading or writing practices. I begin with an example of some of the ideas which emerged from the teaching of a single text: the television play about nuclear war, *Threads*. The main motivation in using this text was that it commanded a great deal of interest and seemed, for obvious reasons, to engage students in a particularly attentive way of watching. The point was certainly not, at least at first, to tackle the nuclear issue, but to put emphasis on a reading of textual production. A number of issues relating to textual production arose from discussions held after the programme had been watched by the whole group. In a production which had put together material from such diverse sources, and which was obviously quoting quite often from external sources – directly in the case of its use of government publications, for example, indirectly in the case of television news format – the relations between intertextual forces and the status granted to the author may be explored. The play (is it a play?) has an author, but also a director and a producer, and has clearly been constructed collectively – as can be evinced from a close analysis of much of the text. In what kind of style, or genre, has the production been cast? Is it, as many would assert, realistic? Is 'realism' the same as 'real'? What elements in the 'play' are there which would encourage us to read it as realistic? What elements might suggest otherwise? Information is flashed onto the screen which at times may claim the status of fact, but which at other times is clearly specu-lation, for example. The 'constructedness' of the programme may be high-lighted by an examination of the deliberate accumulation of metonyms, which follows the initial 'threads' metaphor in the opening sequence. The role, for instance, of the milk-float can be followed by re-running the sections in which it appears. The narrative thread initiated by the metonymically implied moment of conception, and which ends with the ambiguous representation of a birth at the close of the 'film', can be discussed. The sombre music and the serious, male documentary intonation of the voice-over can be identified by students as productive of certain kinds of effects. The kind of people who are portrayed as central characters can be identified as selected – specifically to enhance audience identification.

All of these elements can be identified by students, their local and specific effects discussed and their accumulated effects explored. The question of the cultural specificity of *Threads* as a text dependent on inexplicit reference to so many established conventions from various aspects of television production, can also be discussed and can become part of a more general consideration of television and its use and production of cultural references that shape our ways of seeing things. This phenomenological point, once again, need not be shrouded with any difficult terminology or any especially knotty thinking – but can lead into a consideration of the power of discourses, like the discourse of television in this case, actively working to produce their objects; also, to produce the audience that is capable of consistent, coherent readings, of the object. In the particular case of *Threads*, a whole new dimension may be explored in relation to questions about reader response. The impact of *Threads* is unlikely to have very much that is variable about it, and with fourteen- and fifteen-year-olds is likely to be powerful and disturbing. It's easy to ask what is being disturbed and to explore the ideological composition of what it is that passes for normal life. One of the most interesting opportunities afforded in my own teaching of this text with fourth-years has been discussing with students what happens to this impact once it has passed beyond its initial, shocking phase. How is integration, incorporation, effected without serious disturbance to everyday life? In other words, where does *Threads* go when it's not dominating consciousness?

Fairly straightforward ideas, represented simply, in diagrammatic form on a blackboard, can serve as introductory to a consideration of a psycho-analytic theory of the subject which locates cultural phenomena like *Threads* with a consideration of subjectivity in its relations more generally to culture and to language. Freud's model of the decentred subject, divided between conscious and unconscious and experiencing controlled interchange between the two realms, can be shown to incorporate the idea of repression, the likely contents of the unconscious, the nature of dream experience, the mechanism of censorship, the principles of displacement and condensation. These can all be represented and discussed, and none of it seems to be beyond the competent grasp of fourteen- and fifteen-year-old students.

To this can be added the Lacanian incorporation of language into the Freudian model which emphasizes the construction of the subject and subject positions through the acquisition of language. The splitting of the subject and the relations and differences between the imaginary and symbolic orders and the 'real' can also be described, brought into play and discussed. In the particular case of one fourth-year group, the work they did on *Threads* during their second term was entitled '*Threads* and the Unconscious' and began in most cases with descriptions and diagrams which placed the experience of *Threads* within the ideas they had picked up on subjectivity and its relations to a wider culture that might correspond to ways of understanding the imaginary, symbolic orders and the real, to borrow Lacanian terminology.

The teaching of a single text as described above attempts to highlight the relations between text and extra-textual forces that are at work in the production of textual meaning. The text, in this case, becomes an object of interest itself but is also a pre-text for a more general teaching directed at the understanding of cultural forms and cultural practices in a more theoretical way. One point that was discussed, when dealing with *Threads*, was the context within which it was likely to be viewed. Where would it most likely be watched? What would people be doing while they were watching? What kinds of things might people have been watching before, might they watch after? Does the fact that it is cast in the mode of a narrative television play override other things about it? What difference might these factors make to its impact? The invitation to engage in a contextualizing of media texts emphasizes the determination of the text in its relations with other texts and the social at work in its moment of reception. What happens, though, after the moment of reception? Does the text remain inertly lodged in the conscious or unconscious of individuals? Or is the text talked about, reformulated in some senses and re-read in an important way in the kinds of exchange that are likely to go on about a text with a large audience?

Deconstructing English: discourse analysis

In preparation for extension studies demanded for the GCSE English Literature coursework, one class began a simple exercise in thinking about discourses which became increasingly deconstructive as it progressed. The only thing about these proceedings and their subsequent development which might be considered in the least obscure was the introduction of the word 'taxonomy', which students began to use pretty quickly with facility. The lesson began with the idea of producing a taxonomy of fiction, since it was likely that the extension study for English literature would be concerned with fiction. 'What kinds of fiction are there?' was the opening question, and a list was produced. Departmental policy has been strong for a number of years on a practice of promoting individual reading among students, so that significant time – in most cases a quarter of the time allotted to English – had been dedicated to giving students quiet personal reading sessions, access to the library, opportunities to talk freely among themselves about books they'd read, to accumulate reading capital, to have this recorded by themselves and by their teacher. Much of this reading was their own and not in the possession of the teacher nor subject to the teacher's guiding control. Students had, then, much direct experience of varied fictions.

The point about a taxonomy is that, used in certain ways, it can be made to disrupt exactly what it is supposed to effect; that is, to organize its constituent elements into discrete categories, or to organize clear thought by making distinctions between the essential differences that keep boundaries defined, and to hold orders in order and to stabilize an otherwise shifting and uncertain world. A fiction taxonomy was produced very quickly by '5g':

romance	magazine stories
crime/detective	cheap paperback fiction
war and adventure	extensive paperback fiction
domestic fiction	school library fiction
science fiction	
horror	
	serious fiction
	entertainments
English fiction	literature
Russian fiction	Literature
modern fiction	adult fiction
19th century fiction	teenage fiction
	children's fiction

This taxonomy made it apparent that the world of fiction could not maintain a perfectly stable ordering of its inhabitants. Other factors and forces had to intervene to decide, for instance, the difference between literature and Literature, differences between the prices of types of fiction, between their various audiences. The genre categories were found to be unstable and to have infinite interlinking and overlapping possibilities. Perhaps more seriously for the integrity of the category, the idea that fiction could be constrained to include only novels, or novelettes, or extended prose stories seemed to dissolve all too quickly. Are fictions only contained in books? Is fiction just that kind of writing, those kinds of writing, found on the fiction shelves in libraries or bookshops? Fiction cannot be synonymous with stories. There are other kinds of story which are not fiction. Fiction can't simply be divided from that which is true, either. It might be possible for fiction to represent truth, and it might be the case that what passes for non-fiction – television news stories, documentaries – are highly fictionalized products. What about soap operas, television ads, jokes, anecdotes: what kind of relation do these things have to fiction?

Students will tend to be deeply sceptical of the division between literature and Literature, thinking it falsely social, more probably to do with snobbery and exclusion than absolute value and truth. They will certainly see that the distinction cannot be a property of textual forces alone. And a major move, easily made at this stage, is to make the connection between all the questions, and the uncertainties they gave rise to, about fiction – and what English was all about or could be all about. If a major concern of the subject, English literature, is fiction, if the category fiction itself eludes definition and identity so obviously, doesn't that itself have implications for the identity, integrity and presumptions of the subject which is English? Of course it does; and fourth- or fifth-year comprehensive-school students are as quick to see this point and to understand its implications as sophisticated academics are. There is nothing arcane about this line of thinking and nothing inaccessible about its deconstructive, anti-centric drives, though the academic formulations of similar positions have, unfortunately, tended to shroud themselves in a mystique of difficulty and an exclusive, reference-bound obscurantism which actually obstructs dissemination and which lends such concerns the aura of an excluding practice.

To engage students fully in any discussions which might be dealing with theoretical approaches, to devise activities that enable students to make their own theoretical discoveries, while at the same time letting them know that there are arguments about the issues they're dealing with, that there are differences in the ideology of the subject, that for many the kind of theory they are utilizing is thought to be difficult or rarefied: these approaches are more likely to engender greater confidence than to inspire the terror of inadequacy. Neither the idea of a taxonomy nor the idea of using a taxonomy for deconstructive purposes proved beyond the competence of these students engaged in the topic described above. Once a couple of simple explanations had been given and a full discussion had taken place, students were able to see for themselves the implications and to decide for themselves the kind of position they wanted to adopt in relation to the discussion. This preliminary work certainly enabled them to see more clearly the possibilities for opening up their approaches to the extended, comparative study. They were able to decide with confidence to offer work that, for instance, considered the differences in status between popular and canonical fictions, to give serious consideration to the matter of enjoying texts across a variety of kinds of fiction.

Narratology: stories and truth

More can be done with a more textually focused examination of the structures of fictions and their relationships to readership and to the socially determined production of reading and readings. A scheme of work on the structures of fiction can be initiated by a simple exercise which takes a fiction whose construction is immediately available for analysis. Students are invited to compose a story in not more than, say, sixty words. The story is produced, the author and the audience are ready to hand and, therefore, a more-or-less complete and exhaustive analysis of reading relations can begin. Any number of simple activities are possible which could begin to set familiar habits of reading fiction and ideas about reading fiction into question. In this piece of work it was possible to show how many of our ways of reading, our categories of fiction and our vocabulary of understanding fiction are always constructions that escape the explanation of any given fiction's structural properties.

Once the stories have been written, students may be invited to go on to write or to speak the 'meaning' of their own story. They may also invite another student to read their story and to offer their version of the story's meaning. The two meanings can then be compared. It takes no very complex process to convey to students that the meaning of any text, when examined in this way, is problematic. It becomes quickly apparent that a text is not identical with its meaning; that the meaning of a text is not somehow lodged within it, that the meaning of a text can vary considerably from reader to reader. It is also apparent that the idea of a meaning is in itself a conventional fiction that tends to suppress important aspects of textual relations – such as the social status of the text, the position of the reader, the control of the reading response by the domination of certain conventions. Such conventions tend to read, for instance, certain proper names as indicative of individual character, assumptions of specificity of time and of place, identifications with the strategy of the narrative, the effecting of closure, the suppression of gaps and inconsistencies, and so on.

Students may be invited to join in the collaborative construction of a 'structure box'. Inside the box, which can be drawn as a box in chalk on the board, will go all the elements that go to make up the story: a list that may include features such as beginning, end, middle, title, descriptions, proper names, characters, places, times, and so on. Any one of these can then be taken and examined. Or they can all be taken and applied to any handily available story – fictional or otherwise. The relativity of any one of the terms conventionally used to describe or to catalogue the elements of fiction can be shown to be, at least philosophically, provisional, by suggesting or by providing alternatives. An analysis of 'the symbolic code', for example, in any story would be likely to reveal objects and characters in certain kinds of relation to one another. A function for each, within the strategy of the narrative, could be proffered. Ways of assigning functions to any element, though, will be determined by the kind of reading which is going on. This clearly operates at the level of individual interpretation, but a more radical point can be grasped by students if they are made aware of how kinds of reading themselves – reading practices and positions – are determined by things other than stories or personal idiosyncrasies. A simple introduction of basic terms from phenomenology pointing out the difference between object and aspect may be illuminating in this context, 'the object' here referring to the thing itself, and 'the aspect' referring to the image of the thing itself as seen from a particular viewpoint by a particular viewer. The cultural encoding of meaning – explicitly identified in the work done on gender – can be referred to once again, and examples may be given from stories that inhabit different sectors of cultural space.

One particular example, an item taken from the *Daily Mirror*, 'Treading the Path of Tears', which formed part of a complex text that occupied the first three pages of an issue of the paper, was the basis for a discussion from which a whole section of this work emanated:

Treading the Path of Tears

Jan, a sturdy little police collie, tore into the earth of the haunted moorland wilderness. Dank mud caked her black and white fur as she dug relentlessly into the ground, her finely tuned nose seeking to lay the ghosts of Wildcat Quarry.

For handler Sergeant Neville Sharp, of West Yorkshire police, it was a horror revisited.

He gritted his teeth and held back his fury and tears as his seven-year-old dog scratched furiously into ground that holds secrets and terrors.

Two decades ago he was a young copper assigned to help dig up the mutilated victims of the deranged madness of Myra Hindley and Ian Brady.

He had watched as the bodies were exhumed and taken away.

'I was just a lad at the time', he said yesterday. 'I was so sad, very sad, when I saw those little bodies. I'm a 43-year-old now with two daughters of my own. But I shall never forget what I saw on that awful day.'

Sergeant Sharp is one of the eight-strong sniffer dog team who will be minutely inspecting every blade of grass, every mound of earth and every rock on this desolate moorland called Saddleworth.

It is a disturbingly grim place, hovering above the Dove Stone reservoir.

Little of this bleak landscape has changed since the stomach-churning discoveries that first shook the nation all those years ago.

In the quiet village of Greenfield, just two miles away down a winding muddied road, the people are bracing themselves with grim lips to relive the horrors.

The village pub, The Clarence, is the place where Brady and Hindley calmly and callously played dominoes after their frequent trips to the moors.

It gives you a feeling of chilling eeriness to stand on Hollin Brow Knoll where the abused and tortured body of Lesley Ann Downey had been found.

Or to walk across the charmingly named Isle of Skye road and stare at the earth where the mutilated remains of little John Kilbride were discovered.

'What kind of writing is this?' precipitates the recognition that in this case the factual and the fictional are not clearly textually distinct. The elements which make it seem like a fiction are easily identified. Further questions expose more of the text's use of the conventions of fiction. What role is assigned to the policeman? What role is assigned to the dog? What role is assigned to Brady and Hindley? What is the function, in the 'story', of the village pub? What are the effects intended by the use of the adjectives? Identify them and describe their functions, and so on. What are the effects achieved by the uses and the positionings of place names? All of the elements of the text, their various functions and components, can be shown to be dependent on familiar, culturally common references, showing how this text of uncertain status refers to other commonly available textual forms. Insights gained through this interrogative analytical mode may be further explored and analysed in the process of the students' producing their own similarly-constructed, blatantly inter-textual texts, intermingling the styles of fiction and reality, story and truth. All of this work on the idea of narrative, the idea of the story and the role of the reader and the reading community, might be developed in different directions and in different ways. Once again, the various strands may be brought together by students for an examinable piece of writing. An open structure (organized using a structure box) can be proffered so that students can handle the ideas they're most confident with according to their own ordering.

Closure

English has quite recently discovered its own history, sociology and philosophy. Although this exposure has tended to happen predominantly in the upper academic circle, the movement has at least made available some grounds for transformation in the stalls. It is no longer possible, academically, at least, to maintain a practice of English based on innocence, uncontaminated by theory. That the transformation has not yet occurred on any large or meaningful scale is simply a function of where theory is validated at the moment. Accommodation, appropriation, transformation: of theory itself as well as of English, of the kind of theory now at large which has its own mystifications and exclusivity; resituating theory, liberating and re-distributing it, deprivileging it in spite of its own claims to undermine privilege: these moves might best be effected by its infiltration of the mass medium of English teaching in schools. A reading of 'theory' which makes it accessible to students engaged on GCSE English courses can potentially save the power of theory from its almost hopeless obscurantism, its academic incarceration. This piece has attempted to show that it is possible.

4 'Through a fine web': a post-structuralist approach to working on a text with younger pupils
Cathy Twist

Cathy Twist is Head of English at Stratford School in East London. She is particularly interested in feminist and post-structuralist criticism and says that as she is always running out of ideas for teaching, she has tried to make these theories accessible to her students!

Using post-structuralist 'techniques' for opening up a text to reveal a plurality of meanings has proved rewarding and fruitful for sixth formers. But is the same true for younger pupils? I think so. What follows is an account of a term's work with a mixed-ability, third-year class, from an inner city school, reading *Talking in Whispers* by James Watson, (Victor Gollancz, 1983). The different approach made the text more relevant to the pupils' experience and also gave them a metacode to use when talking about a piece of writing. I began from the premise that the text contained many meanings which could be constructed by the reader, rather than one overall 'message' that has been prescribed by the writer that it is the pupils' job to discover.

Talking in Whispers is a story of oppression in Chile and the courage of the children who fight back. I chose this text because, although difficult, it offers a great deal to readers on a variety of levels.

To briefly summarize the story: Andres Larreta is the son of Juan Larreta, a singer in a group that sang anti-government songs. At the beginning of the story, Andres' father has been killed by the CNI, the Chilean secret police, for political reasons. We also see a rally in a football ground in support of Miguel Alberti, 'The Silver Lion', who it is hoped will become president in the first free elections in Chile for many years. Miguel Alberti is shot dead by the CNI, the elections are cancelled, and a huge police operation is started to wipe out all of his supporters.

During the story, Andres, who is on the run, meets Isa and Beto, who own a travelling puppet show. He becomes friends with them. Isa is a strong character and it is she who successfully initiates most of the children's action.

Andres witnesses many atrocities carried out by the secret police and, through a US journalist who is also killed, gets hold of incriminating photographs of the CNI committing acts of violence and actually shooting 'The Silver Lion'. The children get access to a printing press and reproduce the photographs and manage to get copies out of the country to US newspapers.

Despite everything, the story is very hopeful and the developing relationship between the three children is described beautifully. The puppet shows, the sense of adventure and of success against an enemy, are appealing to most children and can be dealt with alongside the more serious issues.

The story is well written, alternating a clever use of the present tense at the moments when political change seems possible, with sensitive lyrical passages, documentary-style description and realistic dialogue. Resistance songs also play an important role in the story.

We began our post-structuralist approach by talking about the 'frame' or title of the story, *Talking in Whispers*. Pupils made 'word-stars' of thoughts and associations that came to their minds when they read the title. We then pooled these ideas on the blackboard and I wrote them up on a sheet of card as a class poem.

Obviously there were many different ideas, literal and metaphorical, and when we came back to these during and after reading we found ourselves understanding the text on several levels. These were discussed, not formally written down.

Other tasks carried out during reading included finding out specific information about Chile; listening to popular resistance songs that the pupils were familiar with, from U2, Johnny Hates Jazz and John Lennon, as well as some Indian songs that many of the pupils knew well and could translate. (This, incidentally, promoted pupils' positive feelings about their bilingualism.)

After reading the story, which the pupils enjoyed a great deal and also found very challenging, we began to look at it in more detail in order to expose more of what Roland Barthes calls a text's 'facets'.

First we considered our subjective responses and I asked the pupils to write down their thoughts about any aspect of the story. Their work concentrated on the relationships between the children, cruelty, the puppets and the political situation. We read some of these aloud and each version helped pupils to see another person's point of view. They then made posters featuring a picture or diagram and a quotation from the book that they felt summed up their viewpoint.

We then concentrated on the 'structural metaphor' of the whole story: what was the deep dynamic meaning as opposed to the superficial meaning? To do this pupils got into mixed discussion groups and talked for about fifteen minutes. Then a spokesperson reported back to the class. Most children decided that it was the power of love against almost anything else which was the deepest 'meaning' of the story. Love for humanity in general and for truth as well as for individuals: 'Love is not something that gets smaller if you divide it up.' This was a sophisticated response and we discussed what this notion meant to the pupils in their lives. This led on to a discussion about sibling jealousy and friendship. The pupils then wrote a brief passage from James Watson's point of view entitled 'Why I wrote the book'. This exercise developed still more possible angles of vision on the text.

We looked at two passages from the book in detail: one where Isa and Beto talk about their love for each other and the possible threat of Andres entering their relationship, and one where Andres is being tortured by the CNI. We looked at the effect these passages have on each other, in other words, how contiguous links in the story are effective or illuminating. The pupils then chose other contrasting words, ideas and phrases and considered what effect they have on each other and the reader.

We considered which were the most dominant or recurring ideas and words. Pupils made lists in pairs. Most went for the 'action' type ideas and the more lyrical words dealing with emotions. This again threw up some interesting paradoxes which are an inherent part of the book.

Looking at the dyadic oppositions and the cultural codes in the story was more difficult for the pupils. We looked at the book first in terms of the obvious power structure in Chile as it is described, headed by the Junta and General Zuckermann. We then thought about who *we* felt should be in control and of course turned the whole structure on its head. This was quite an extended task which involved the pupils' filling in grids to show hierarchies of power of the two kinds. At the end of the discussions and group work, pupils could see that the real power in the text is located with the children, the reporter and the underground movement. This was a particularly fruitful focus of interest that the pupils could finally come to terms with only by looking at the *words* James Watson uses to describe the power of the CNI and the power of Andres, Isa and Beto. This led on to a discussion of power in their own relationships; the 'power' of bullies and the 'power' of loyalty.

We considered the vehicles for language in the text – what the writer says or implies about writing in the writing, the 'metacode'. To do this the pupils were asked to see how many styles of writing are used; how the writer describes *how* ideas and messages are passed on; what is the power of words? Here we discovered a power that even the CNI were afraid of: the Western press. We enumerated newspapers, poems, songs of resistance, illegal broadsheets and word of mouth. We looked at who the first people to be arrested were: they were those who dealt with words in their professions – teachers, poets, journalists, and so on. Pupils realized for themselves the power of language; to back up this work we looked at some broadsheets that were going around the school at that time and at a news article reported differently in different newspapers. This led to holding a debate entitled 'Talking in Whispers is banned', which was very successful.

Looking at the characters in the book took up several weeks. We considered the roles of men, women, boys and the girl Isa. Pupils observed the characters' differing responses to crises. It was interesting for pupils to note that Isa was the one who was in control most of the time, even though initially they had noticed no difference between the children's behaviour.

This challenged some of their gender stereotyping, as did Beto's open response of jealousy to his sister's developing affection for Andres.

Ways of maintaining pupil involvement in the story while we were reading included prediction exercises and role-play. One of the most successful was getting pupils to imagine they were Andres in prison; I gave them all a piece of paper and told them I was the jailer (!), I walked round the room and each of them had to try and scribble a message to Isa and Beto without my seeing them writing. They enjoyed this and it also reinforced the message about the power of language and the importance of communication.

The visual imagery of the book is very powerful and the pupils illustrated various parts of the story. They then swapped pictures and wrote a descriptive passage stimulated by each others' pictures.

I briefly introduced them to the concept of the 'social relations' of the text: is the author the same as the narrator? Does the narrator share all the protagonists' points of view? How might this book be read by a child in Chile, or in South Africa? Is it different for different people in the class? Why?

During the term's work on *Talking in Whispers* the class wrote long prose pieces, poetry, did some drama, drew pictures and discussed many issues. Although many of the approaches were initiated by me, pupils controlled their own learning and instigated much of the discussion. They also began to understand how to be confident critics and how to talk about language.

This essay only describes the response of one age-group of pupils to one text, but I found that making use of simplified post-structuralist methods was far more enriching and creative than a didactic approach, largely because the text is opened up in so many different ways and allows pupils a variety of viewing points from which to consider and respond to the issues it raises.

5 Teasing out 'The Tyger': exploring reading strategies with second-years

Paul Bench

Paul Bench teaches English and Drama at Wrockwardine Wood School, Telford, where he is Head of Year and Language Co-ordinator. He works for the Board of The London Academy of Music and Dramatic Art assessing candidates to Performer and Teaching Diploma levels. His research study has been in theoretical interpretation and the role of the reader.

There is perhaps in all of us an endless yearning for static, once-and-for-all meaning. The desire to make an equation and to close the book on it forever. How our pupils long for us sometimes to dictate, with the authoritative might of the teacher, the answer beneath the text, to open the sealed evelope of meaning as one might at some theatrical Oscar-giving ceremony!

All the probing is finished, the arguments concluded, the pen may now write on the paper, the examiner satisfied and distributing his confetti of marks. The pain gone. For reading and encountering may be painful and disturbing. The disturbance when the reading of words touches a nerve ending in the reader, when a text jolts thought and feelings into action. When your conscious and unconscious and all that you are as a human being is summoned to move.

It is disturbing for the teacher. To issue notes, to throw chocolate drops of knowledge and received wisdom into the wide open mouths of calling pupils is a tempting, beckoning finger. How much time it saves!

Pupils have sometimes said to me, 'You are the teacher, you've studied English, and you should know the answers. Can't you just tell us what Romeo's character is like?' In the good old days I suppose I would have done. When I joined in the conspiracy of keeping the text pure. Saved the text from the smudge of the adolescent's aberrant thought-processes.

There is nothing, of course, intrinsically wrong about familiarizing readers with the insights of great literary critics into particular works of literature, but what purpose will this serve unless some form of personal encounter has been

31

made between reader and text? I do not simply mean a cognitive encounter, but a complete meeting and fusion of the reading personality, with the reader as a real person and not just as a brain or intellect.

Stanley Fish says, 'I would go so far as to say that what it [a text] does, is what it means.'[1] But what does a text do? What exactly is a text? In very bold terms, it is no more than black markings on a page. Who shall ever know what authorial intention these clusters of signifiers, to use Saussure's terminology, are designed to express? What if the author is long dead, or has forgotten what she or he meant?

The field of reader reception theory, of post-structuralism and semiotics, is a vast treasure-trove to plunder. Of one thing there may be some certainty, that without the *individual* reader, a text is no more than ink spots on paper. If the reader, in our case the young reader, does not have a personal agenda with the text, then the text is of no importance.

In this chapter I wish to examine some recent theorists' considerations and to suggest some ways in which they may be of practical help in literature teaching. Far from being academic abstractions more suited to the university seminar, these considerations may illuminate the dynamics of the process of reading and the reception of literature in the classroom.

I am going to take an example of a specific, well-known text, 'The Tyger' by William Blake. This is a text which I offered to some comprehensive secondary-school pupils in the second year and of mixed-ability grouping. I wanted the pupils to enjoy the poem as personal readers for the first time without any direct teacher intervention in terms of meaning or critical analysis. My intention was that they should meet the poem in a variety of ways, as individuals, as group participants, and as readers using not just intellect but the complete psyche. I wanted to prompt the entire engine of the reading process into play.

In the first instance I read the poem to them without providing a copy of the text. I read it to them a second and third time, on each occasion with slightly different emphasis and approach. I read it with great feeling and sense of dramatic occasion, colouring the phrases vocally and pacing the reading in a structured way. I then read the poem in a somewhat humorous way, deliberately encouraging a response which took the grandeur out of the Tiger. I finally read in a more distant controlled way, toning, down the vocal colouring and sense of occasion.

Finally I invited willing readers to read the poem to groups of three or four pupils who arranged their own choice. Copies of the poem were provided at this juncture.

My purpose in this was to avoid as much as possible any preset interpretation or response. The pupils heard the poem through the medium of other readers but with different emphases. Also, they were being familiarized with the sounds of the poem, with its words and phrasing. They then read the poem on the page.

I asked all poems to be turned over and requested the pupils not to look at the words, however tempting it might be. They then wrote down on paper any thoughts, memories, associations and reactions to the idea of Tiger, and any words or phrases that the poem 'Tyger' left in their minds.

I wanted to invite a kaleidoscopic cauldron of images and impressions on the idea of Tiger, a cubist jungle of words. I was applying some of the notions of post-structuralist thought exemplified by Roland Barthes. Barthes would dissolve meaning totally as an apprehensive commodity into one intense pleasure of flickering linguistic recognitions. He invites the reader to participate in the 'jouissance', the sensual playfulness, of the text.

The pupils were asked to jot down words in a haphazard way, to let them spread over the page in any form. To take one example, Kathy's page had the following items:

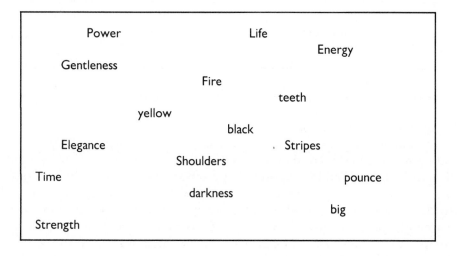

As a piece of homework, each pupil was asked, irrespective of their ability at drawing, to assemble the essence of Tiger and 'The Tyger' into a collation of drawn images. No marks were to be awarded for drawing skills but the pupils were simply requested to transpose into another medium a distillation of all that 'tigeriness' suggested to them emotionally and intellectually. Some of the results of these were of considerable fascination to me as the teacher.

Matthew's drawing presented a realistic pencil-etched tiger with an Esso can of petrol on his back. The tiger itself was surrounded by tongues of fire from which emerged a nuclear warhead with USA marked clearly upon it and a powerful machine gun protruded from the tiger's tail. The tiger was stepping over an Inter City railway diesel engine and its left hind leg was manacled by chains to a devil's three-pronged fork. Most significantly, around the tiger's head was a halo. Two flags, one with stars and stripes and another with hammer and sickle, penetrate the flames, crossing each other. Other drawn images in pupils' presentations took the form of cars, trains, electric light bulbs, suns, torches, a huge prison door, hammer and nails.

It was at this point that we were able to turn to a variety of post-structuralist approaches to enquire further into our understanding of Blake's poem.

Binary relationships

It has been argued by Jakobson and Saussure that the composition and construction of language is essentially bound by oppositions. All concepts are defined by relating them to their opposites. The basic semiotic model according to Greimas[2] to which all narrative conforms is the relationship between two opposites and two negatives.

Example	
Life/Death	Life/Non-Life

thus the formula

A : B	: :	–A : –B

All stories are generated in this way.

The pupils were asked in pairs to make quick brief notes of all the oppositions and contrasts that they were able to observe in 'Tyger'. They should include both literal and metaphorical oppositions. We had already discussed metaphor and they were therefore familiar with this as a literary device. I worked with one pupil who had the previous year received additional learning support in English. For fun we decided to see which pair could compile the longest list, although no great emphasis was given to the final result. I list below some of the suggestions of these pupils which they put forward in subsequent class discussion:

Tears : smiling	terror : joy
burning bright : night	deeps : skies
hand : feet	brain : heart
Lamb : tiger	calmness : ferocity
heaven : hell	water : fire
light : shade	night : day
mortal : immortal	Fear : courage
noise : quiet	spears : tears
hard : soft	violence : gentleness
grasping : letting go	strength : weakness
muscles : brain	weapons : peace
God : Satan	Good : Bad
forests : furnace	

In the following lesson I pushed the class into the deeper quarry which Jonathan Culler outlines as the three conventions of Literary Competence:

> the rule of significance
> metaphorical coherence
> thematic unity

According to Culler,[3] an effective reader of Literature needs to be able to grasp these three conventions. I had no intention of using this form of technical expression, but I wanted the pupils to internalize very simply the grammar of literature.

The pupils' drawings had already suggested some unconscious grasp of these notions and I therefore asked them to discuss in small groups in what ways the tigers could be considered in a metaphorical sense and in what ways they had already seen them so used.

I visited each group in turn and listened to some of the suggestions that they had noted down:

> Tiger in the petrol tank expressing amazing power and energy

> Tigers as rugby players expressing strength and vitality, muscularity and masculinity

(An absorbing tangent to discussion then arose over what masculinity and feminity really were. Again our thoughts about opposites and contrasts played a significant role, where some fierce opposition was expressed by the girls, who resented the idea that femininity was only portrayed as soft, gentle, kind and submissive.)

> Tiger as the Sun

(Two of the pupils' drawings had already depicted the face of a tiger framed within a burning sun.)

> Tiger as God
> Tiger as the Devil
> Tiger as uncontrolled instinct in mankind
> Tiger as playful, natural part of our personalities

(Reference was made to Winnie the Pooh's Tigger, to considerable amusement.)

It was at this point and in the ensuing lesson that ideas were put forward about metaphorical images within the poem, of the furnace and vast blacksmith's shop of Life where power and machinery, the engine-room of human effort, is to be found. We decided that was both an exciting and dangerous place. It was a power-house for good and evil in much the same way as is perhaps nuclear energy.

I drew attention to the rhythm of the poem, which has an energy and a flow to it, and a constant metrical beat, and asked them if they saw significance in this respect. Some pupils suggested the beat of the Tiger's heart, others the rhythmical beat of machinery, others the beating of the hammers.

Such points as were emerging from discussion were, of course, illuminating, but I was anxious that the pupils should relate their thoughts to themselves and to life in general as they perceived it.

Wolfgang Iser[4] employs the term 'Repertoire' to express two points about the reading.

a) The Repertoire contained in the text

b) The Repertoire that a reader brings to the text.

The repertoire of the text is the common assumptions, cultural and historical, held by both reader and text. The reader brings to the text his or her own personal experiences, upbringing and psychology and the chemistry brings the words on the page to life. In other words, what the reader brings to the text is the substance of aesthetic responses.

Personal experience is essential to create textual meaning and pupils should be made aware of this and be encouraged to use their own lives to bring the text to life. This point of view has echoes in Roland Barthes' exposition of Reader Codes, to which I shall shortly refer.

I set two tasks to elicit a more immediate personal response, one 'compulsory' as a short piece of written work, the other optionally as a tape recording for homework.

The written work was to respond to the title 'The Tiger in me'. We had already in a previous project on Faces considered the opposites in ourselves as personalities, the different and sometimes unpredictable qualities we show as people.

These were not meant to be particularly polished assignments, merely short working documents to help pupils to find a niche from which to climb on to the wheel of the text. Images of energy, sporting activities, aggressive assertions, were frequently recurring patterns in the pupils' writing:

'The Tiger comes out of me when I swim and ride my bike. Swimming, I just go faster and faster as if I'm exhausted then I must go on with determination like the tiger.'

'There is a tiger in me at night. I used to be afraid of the dark but now I just feel quite safe as if there's a tiger in me protecting me.'

'Tiger, Tiger, burning bright, like me when getting angry, more and more all the time. Flames getting higher and higher and ready to explode.'

Four or five pupils requested to do the tape recording. One girl, Heather, interestingly read the poem through the microphone before giving her personal responses, whilst in the background a rhythmic click echoed the metre. Some of the points which Heather made in her responses were centred on the similarity between Man and Tiger and a plea that tigers should be left alone and unhunted by mankind.

Mark's thoughts were concerned with ideas of Heaven and Hell, 'God and the Devil fighting against each other all the time.' He went on to consider the strength and power of the tiger and yet how 'easy it glides over the surface of the plains.'

Within these small seedbeds of thought, it seems to me, are the beginnings of a more distanced, reflective, critical assessment. They need some nurture and elaboration which I hope in time will develop in the pupils as reflective readers gradually immersing themselves in the language of poetics.

I do not at this stage particularly wish my pupils to be obsessed by an endless search for meaning, but to experience poetry and words and language in a highly pluralistic way.

Barthes comments: 'What takes place in a narrative is, from the referential point of view, literally nothing; what happens is language alone '[5] and Susan Sontag suggests that we should free ourselves of an endless slavery of interpretation: 'Interpretation takes the sensory experience of the works of art for granted, and proceeds from there . . . what is important now is to recover our senses. We must learn to *see* more, to *hear* more, to *feel* more.'[6]

We may not necessarily hold completely with these views but it does seem to me to be important that young readers learn to participate in the game of the text, to work with the author in a variety of ways. Their entire selves, their experience, their knowledge, their feelings, enable the text to be actualized. In Iser's terms, they fill in the gaps, recreate the text for themselves imaginatively. Or, as Norman Holland from the psychoanalytic school quotes Edgar Hyman, 'Each reader poems his own Poems.'[7]

The Codes of Roland Barthes

Barthes has argued in his book *S/Z* (see bibliography) that a literary text is sectioned together in a structure of codes, which he then applies to an analysis of Balzac's story, *Sarrasine*. He identifies five codes from an indefinite possible number of codes to which the units of a book are applied. It is with the aid of these codes that Barthes provides the reader with freedom from tyranny of the text. Most pupils of reasonable reading ability and experience are likely to have a clear understanding of the codes unconsciously, but I think it is important to make this knowledge more conscious.

I want my pupils to have a more active awareness of ways in which they can exploit these codes in their reading. In other words, they must help themselves to recode the text, to recreate it through the sort of knowledge they are able to bring to reading. In the activities I have described with young 12- to 13-year-old mixed-ability pupils, the codes were used in obvious ways unconsciously.

The semic code

The understanding of characters, both of those in the text (in our case 'The Tyger') and of those whom we meet generally in our lives. Positive and negative characteristics should be noted by pupils. I ask my pupils to note down any adjectives which describe personality and motive. Do they confirm or disrupt assumptions which have already been made?

The proairetic code

To understand how actions influence events. What consequences result. Pupils need to be encouraged to see how one event influences another, in other words, the significance and insignificance of actions. In 'The Tyger', for example, the alteration of the word 'could' to 'dare' in the first and last three verses was highlighted by pupils. We then discussed the events of the poem, the segments of thought that had led the text to this apparently minor exchange of vocabulary which, on greater scrutiny, is a pivot for the entire poem. Reviewing the text between those two verses helps the reader to see how the varying segments of thought and ideas hold the poem together by binary oppositions of theme or symbol.

The hermeneutic code

To explore mysteries and puzzles in the text. The setting up of hypotheses, the enjoyment of searching for meaning and of realizing that the surface appearance of the texts may belie the more complicated and absorbing meaning not immediately apparent.

Pupils' use of the hermeneutic code will involve the fascination of searching for clues and the satisfaction that results in trying to sort out problems within a text. In this way the multilinear threads of meaning and narrative are brought to attention, and the constant flickering of meanings identified by Barthes appreciated.

The symbolic code

To search for patterns expressing theme and meaning through the use of symbol.

Barthes describes this code as one saliently concerned with use of contrasts. Once a contrast has been detected, pupils may be asked to search for all ideas, texts both referential and associative, that may be listed under each of the two contrasting points or themes.

Language as a symbol, as a means of expressing plurality of meaning is highlighted. Thus a more easy entry may be made into puzzling areas of texts and an understanding of the way that language is never singular in what it says, but multi-faceted, is encouraged.

The second-year pupils latched quickly on to this, bringing their own experience of symbol, such as the Esso petrol tiger, or tiger rugby team, to explore the richer avenues of meaning in the poem.

The cultural code

To see how knowledge and experience of different societies, age groups, sex, cultures, everyday knowledge and specialist knowledge, may be used to explore variations in meaning.

It is through this code that the author, almost confidentially, speaks to the reader in subtle ways, drawing upon a shared cultural understanding of life.

It is a particularly useful code to bring to the pupils' attention because it serves to free the text from the hemmed-in, culture-bound meaning imposed frequently and unconsciously by the author's cultural assumptions.

Some breaking down of these barriers was achieved by the pupils reading 'The Tyger'. We asked whether tigers are only aggressive and dangerous as we commonly assume, and discussion led us as a group to consider the softer, purring and playful side of tigers and tiger cubs.

A useful strategy of presenting this bondage of text to the reader is to ask pupils to read the words as if from the point of view of a reader from a totally different culture or planet, or from a different age in history. What areas of meaning and suggestion would be foreign and closed to them?

These uses of Barthes' codes of literature were employed unconsciously by the young readers we have been considering, although they were consciously led to exploring them by myself as the teacher. As they progress to become more informed readers, I am suggesting that they should be more consciously made aware of their function. It seems that areas of literature remain closed to so many young people and that their dependency on teachers and lecturers is increased because of their lack of initiation and of confidence into the 'secrets' of the reading agenda.

In this chapter I have been at pains to explain how the abstruse and perplexing arena of modern literary theory is not simply a playground for deconstructionist academics. The 'game' of reading and interpretation is one which is frequently closed to the young and inexperienced reader, and those who have learnt the rules unconsciously participate in the conspiracy of keeping those rules aloof from others. Reader response theory applies an X-ray through the skin of the reading process, revealing the network of its veins and its nervous system.

> They've taken the skeleton
> Of the great Irish Elk
> Cut up the peat, set it up
> An astounding crate full of air
>
> Every layer they strip
> Seems camped on before
> The bogholes might be Atlantic seepage
> The wet centre is bottomless.
>
> (Seamus Heaney, *Bogland*)[8]

NOTES

1   S. Fish, 'Literature in the Reader: Affective Stylistics', in *Is There a Text in This Class?*, Harvard University Press, 1980.

2   A. J. Greimas, *Semantique Structurale*, Paris, Larousse, 1966.

3   J. Culler, *Structuralist Poetics: Structuralism, Linguistics and the Study of Literature*, London, Routledge and Kegan Paul, 1975.

4   W. Iser, *The Act of Reading: A Theory of Aesthetic Response*, London, Johns Hopkins University Press, 1978.

5   R. Barthes, *Image–Music–Text*, trs. S. Heath, London, Fontana, 1977.

6   S. Sontag, 'Against Interpretation' in *20th Century Literary Criticism*, D. Lodge, ed., London, Longman, 1972.

7   N. Holland, *Five Readers Reading*, London, Yale University Press, 1975.

8   S. Heaney, *Door Into The Dark*, London, Faber & Faber, 1969.

6 Gender issues at A Level: a classroom perspective

Margaret Whiteley

Margaret Whiteley has been Head of the Language and Literature Faculty at Shena Simon College in Manchester for six years. Before that she worked in comprehensive schools in Rochdale and Manchester. She believes that change is very much on the agenda for A Level English, and that is the starting point for this article.

Like many English teachers of the late sixties and early seventies, educated in the Leavisite tradition, I began teaching an A Level English Literature syllabus identical to the one I had taken as a sixth-former. Early in my teaching career, I felt dissatisfied with the Great Traditional syllabus and I was not alone; dissatisfaction has been expressed since much earlier this century.[1] One of my early ideas about change at A Level centred on the notion of 'breaking the silence'; I was strongly impressed by the work of feminists who at that time were demonstrating how many women writers had been stifled by male critics paying virtually exclusive attention to male writers. While I still believe that it's important to uncover previously unknown writers, the work of publishers like Virago and the Women's Press has at least made them more accessible to the public, and thus effected an important raising of consciousness. Any choice of texts for examination purposes is politically loaded and highlights the problem of whether choosing texts by women writers endows them with that seal of approval that Adrian Mitchell so strongly objected to when one of his poems was set on the then 16 Plus paper.

The other problem of course is that adding a few more texts by women doesn't alter the theoretical assumptions on which traditional literary-critical approach exams depend. The arguments about the shortcomings of A Level Literature syllabuses have been well-rehearsed elsewhere and I do not want to repeat them now.[2] I mention the issue because it forced me to work out classroom practice which was based on sound theoretical premises which took into account the issues being raised in relation to English as an academic discipline.

One of my main aims as an English teacher has always been to develop students' 'language control',[3] to move students from being passive recipients of information to becoming active makers and participants in the educational process. I recognize that there is nothing radical or new in this aim, but it did not accord with my experience of the demands made by the A Level Literature syllabus I was teaching, and it certainly didn't accord with the experience of the large number of girls I taught. (At the sixth-form college where I now work, girls on A Level English courses outnumber boys by almost 3:1.) Research has shown that boys dominate in classroom interaction and the message girls receive throughout their school lives is that they should be quiet, well-mannered and well-presented.[4] I shall suggest later ways in which the research findings themselves can be investigated by students as part of a process of active learning.

Precisely this process informs the 'investigation into the nature and function of language' of the JMB's A Level English Language (public since 1988), in which linguistic theory underpins practice but does not necessitate prescriptive constraints. It is in this context that I want to consider the way feminism might affect classroom practice in both language and literature courses. My first impulse is in fact to offer a disclaimer about the relationship between feminism and its place in literary and linguistic theory. It's important, I think, not to regard feminism as simply a kind of alternative theory or system; it comes from what approximately half the population *is*. Having made this disclaimer, though, it's also important to recognize that theorizing about female experience is necessary if we are to analyse the social conventions that shape our experience.

Looking at the large number of books available on feminist literary theory quickly indicates that there is no single line of feminist thought and it is evident that feminism has drawn on, for example, Marxism, structuralism, psychoanalysis and deconstruction. The recent *Feminist Literary Theory: A Reader*, edited by Mary Eagleton, offers an overview of developments and relationships, and it is just these relationships that persuade me to see feminism as having a unique impact and position.

The multiplicity of theoretical critical positions can seem intimidating; it can equally be enriching if you accept pluralism as positively beneficial. But I agree with Mary Eagleton when she says in her Preface to *Feminist Literary Theory* that she wants to reach a wider audience than an exclusively academic, Higher Education one. I certainly want to reach an audience of students at pre-HE stage, though most books about feminist theory (with the possible exception of Dale Spender's *Man Made Language*, (Routledge and Kegan Paul, 1980) are addressed to adult readers and written from an adult, and usually an academic, perspective.

We also have to face the fact that the term 'feminist' has had a bad press, causing students to suffer a variety of misconceptions. So perhaps we have to be canny and use humour, tact and sensitivity – such as we might want to inculcate in our students, and indeed, in our opponents too – to overcome prejudice and intolerance.

Reaching the classroom can initially depend on tacit strategies, aimed more at heightening awareness than actually addressing the gender issue head-on. But what we order for the school library, books in the classroom, what we choose to display of students' work, books and pictures we use for decorating the classroom, can all convey implicit messages about what we value and think worthwhile. Inviting women writers into schools and colleges under Arts Council funded schemes is not too expensive and again reinforces positive images. While choice of texts for exams is a political minefield, the more texts by women are available to students, the better. Syllabuses offering coursework options are gaining in popularity,[5] so individually negotiating choices with students becomes not only desirable but possible and practical.

These measures are not enough. There are still many who think gender issues are peripheral to the real business of education. They are not. Women encounter prejudice whether they recognize it or not, and we have to find ways of confronting it and dealing with it. As teachers, I believe we have the same responsibility towards highlighting sexism as we have towards doing the same for racism.

In so far as language shapes our experience, it's evident that gender stereotyping exists from the outset. Choice of clothing or toys for young children reinforces strong social messages about gender divisions, and helps to establish behaviour patterns. Early experience of books, too, indicates reluctance to abandon the familiar domestic, passive roles for mother and daughter, and the active, socially important roles for father and son. Although valiant attempts to counteract this have been made, I am equally aware that some of my students were taught to read by the same reading scheme that I was brought up on over thirty years ago – Janet and John – so it's not difficult to see how it becomes necessary to make a conscious effort to resist the effects of such stereotyping. This is what I try to achieve with my students.

One obvious example of contemporary sexism can be found in cartoon strips like 'Andy Capp' and 'Jane'. Even allowing for the legitimate satirical dimension, it's easy enough to find examples of crude assumptions about gender roles (for instance, the nagging wife, mother-in-law jokes, the busty barmaid, and so on) where language will reflect and reinforce the visual image. Exploring the connotations of terms characterizing women's language can be the next stage. 'Gossip', 'bitching about', 'tittle-tattle', all have pejorative overtones and further implications to lead perhaps into the area of folk-linguistic beliefs like the popular notion that men swear more than women. Students can research this folk wisdom by designing questionnaires. This in itself requires a degree of rigour, but can be adapted to suit the level of students' operation. Conducting research to test the results of the questionnaire is an obvious extension, but this is likely to involve fearless treks around local pubs, armed with tape recorders . . . not always a wise course. Despite background noise and lack of clarity, the most fruitful information can usually be gleaned from students' peer groups.

Some discourse analysis could also be incorporated into examining success-ful recordings. Positions adopted by men talking together tend to be com-petitive and aggressive, whereas women are more inclined to co-operative and supportive exchanges. Their findings can be compared with those of academic researchers,[6] and here is a way to introduce students to academic texts which might otherwise seem intimidating if approached 'cold'. It is important to stress at this point, though, the scientific rigour of experiments conducted by those whose livelihood derives from research.

At some point, students also need to become familiar with the social network theory, as advanced by, for instance, Milroy.[7] The theory could be tested at a simple level by studying a closely-knit social peer group as enforcing varieties of non-standard usage. This could serve as an introduction to the more sophisticated research carried out by Leslie Milroy and described very clearly by Jennifer Coates in *Women, Men and Language,* suggesting that gender is not the dominant factor in the well-documented evidence that women use more prestige norms – the spoken standard dialect – than men, but the strength of the social network to which someone belongs.

Teacher and students can have lots of fun with generic pronouns. Tracing the origins of the male as the inclusive norm, in relation to other aspects of language change is very revealing. So is trying out the semantic shifts when the generic 'he' is replaced by the female variety. Analysing such utterances as, 'When God made men She was only joking' can reveal much about the attitudes of those involved in the discussion. Try replacing other famous sayings with female pronouns; Ellen Moers[8] has subverted many famous literary statements with this device.

Media representations of women are an obvious source for examples of blatant sexism. I shan't apologize for the obviousness since, while the tactics of, say, the *Sun* may be clear to us as teachers, I have not yet encountered one student who has rigorously examined the language of the press in presenting gender stereotypes. Even in articles of serious news, women are described in terms of physical appearance. The clichés are apparent and can be exploited in trivializing women's validity and value. So turn the tables and apply some to famous men. How do they look as a result of this treatment? The blatant sexism of the *Sun* also has its more subtle counterpart in the quality press, often of the type used by the judge who described Mary Archer, the wife of the plaintiff in a libel case, as 'fragrant'.

Advertising is another obvious area to quarry. Juxtaposing visual images of men with bodice-ripping copy makes an immediate impact and is fun to do. Involving students in making these stylistic choices helps them to focus on the underlying assumptions about the audience at whom the originals are directed.

Magazines aimed at a male audience (not the pornographic variety!) make an interesting comparison to the standard women's magazine, and concentrating on one specific area, such as fiction, highlights some revealing linguistic choices . . . and prevents accusations of exclusively female concerns.

In general, however, I would argue that it does no harm for males to experience a sense of exclusion. It might help them to understand how women have felt for a long time. In the classroom I would exercise this carefully as I do not want to fall into the trap of playing men's games by manipulating a power relationship.

My intention is that all this data should help students to formulate a view of how cultural stereotypes are formed. It might be instructive to investigate the strategies employed as conscious efforts to redress the balance. A quite simple device like the introduction of 'Ms' is still riddled with misconceptions. At least eight out of a group of ten girls in 1987 thought the title was used only by those who had been divorced or who didn't want to admit that they weren't married! Students could work on the task of suggesting future linguistic tactics to dispel folk beliefs about gender. Rewriting children's readers is a popular exercise. Trying to find alternatives for patriarchal last names involves imagination and ingenuity – and no one has solved this particular problem yet.

In a more specifically literary framework, there is much to be examined. I am here using the term literature with a lower-case 'l' and even traditional Literature syllabuses allow space for exploration beyond the confines of the Canon.

I am aware that many teachers disapprove of what is often referred to as 'pulp' fiction. But I think it is important for us to understand the massive popularity of the romance novel without making those who read them feel ridiculed. Alison Light[9] has suggested that we should 'develop a rigorous and compassionate understanding' about the place these novels may hold in some women's lives, while challenging their stereotypical qualities, and making this an opening to rechannel 'the dissatisfactions on which [the novels] depend.' For we should avoid participating in what Adrienne Rich describes as using literature against students 'to keep them in their place, to mystify, to bully, to make them feel powerless.'[10] This is why we need to take seriously where the student is in her reading, and start from there.

It's not a bad idea to expose some of the men writing authoritatively about women, who make the same assumptions about women that I have been attempting to dispel in this piece, but whose work has been validated by academic approval. D.H. Lawrence springs immediately to mind; there are other examples.

Let's not overlook positive representations in fiction either. Jane Austen and George Eliot will have their place here, and so will many contemporary writers, both those who call their writing feminist and those who don't. I would recommend Jane Rogers' *Her Living Image* (Faber, 1984) and *Separate Tracks* (Faber, 1983), Jeanette Winterson's *Oranges are not the only Fruit* (Pandora, 1985), any of Fay Weldon's short stories, anything of Alice Walker's, and Grace Nichols' and Gillian Clarke's poetry.

Reflecting on texts for herself will help the student gain access to and ownership of the writing. And students' own writing can be a powerful part of that process. Why not attempt fiction that tries to exemplify Cheri Register's[11] prescriptive notions about what feminist writing should be:

> To earn feminist approval, literature should perform one or more of the following functions:

1) serve as a forum for women
2) help to achieve cultural androgyny
3) provide role-models
4) promote sisterhood
5) augment consciousness-raising

It may well be that these strictures are impossible and even undesirable, but they would be interesting ones to try out with students.

Another notion to test might be the question of whether it is possible for men to write convincingly of female experience, or to use the female viewpoint at all.

Would it be possible to adopt the formulae of romantic novels and subvert them to feminist ends?

Possibilities for creating fictions abound and I'm sure I don't need to rehearse what may sound like old chestnuts to some readers. I hope some of these old chestnuts, though, are worth collecting and preserving.

After several weeks' work on gender and language recently, one of my students articulated her response to what she'd learnt in this way: 'It makes you think about things you've always taken for granted and begin to question them.' It may not be the revolution, but it's a start.

I've tried to demonstrate how issues of gender are not optional extras in education, pre- or post-sixteen, but that if we are to develop fully all students' potential and give them the education they're entitled to, these issues must be addressed as a matter of urgency and priority.

NOTES

1 See, for instance, *Curriculum and Examinations in Secondary Schools* 1943, the report of a national committee under Sir Cyril Norwood. And John Dixon in *Schools Council 16–19 Project: The Role of English and Communication*, Macmillan, 1975.

2 See, for example, *English A-level in Practice*, NATE, 1988.

3 David Jackson, *Continuity in Secondary English*, Methuen, 1982.

4 Examples of classroom research are quoted in *Gender Issues in English Coursework*, NATE, 1988.

5 See Bill Greenwell, *Alternatives at A-level*, NATE, 1988.

6 Jennifer Coates, *Women, Men and Language*, Longman, 1986.

7 Lesley Milroy, *Language and Social Networks*, Basil Blackwell, 1980.

8 In *Literary Women*, Women's Press, 1978.

9 Alison Light, article in *Feminist Review*, quoted in Mary Eagleton, ed., *Feminist Literary Theory: A Reader*, Basil Blackwell, 1986, p.144.

10 Adrienne Rich, *On Lies, Secrets and Silence*, Virago, 1980, p.63.

11 Cheri Register, article in *Feminist Literary Criticism*, quoted in Eagleton, ed., *Feminist Literary Theory*, pp. 169–70.

7 Dialogues on *The Color Purple*
Gill Murray and Val Fraser

Gill Murray is Head of English at Bramcote Park Comprehensive School, near Nottingham. Val Fraser is second in English at Rufford Comprehensive, Edwinstone. Both have been increasing their acquaintance with, and respect for, critical theory over the last five or six years, but were somewhat sceptical about its direct application in the classroom. It was finally through an involvement in gender initiatives in Nottinghamshire that they saw the potential for using approaches from critical theory in working with A Level texts in the Associated Examining Board's 660 syllabus. Their aim was to explore the structural constraints placed upon women and men by the oppression of sex, race and class, and to locate the possibilities of emancipation in the work of a Black woman writer.

I Gill Murray's account

I was nudged in the direction of attempting something different with this text by several factors. First of all it was a rather tricky, possibly unsuitable text to do with this particular class. They were not a harmonious group, hardly knew one another before the start of the year, and lessons were often slow and edgy, with the two brightest boys saying very little (unless it was deflecting or negative) and the other five (two boys and three girls) generally anxious, quiet and wary; I had never taught a class where so little collaborative learning or interaction took place or where discussion was so halting. I had had to choose and order texts, however, before meeting the group and I was interested to see how they would cope. I launched into Alice Walker's *The Color Purple* in January of their Lower VI year, without a great deal of optimism, but thinking that at least they might find it a welcome change from their previous course-work text, *Twelfth Night*. Additionally, it offered some interesting connections with their first text, *Klute* – I imagined all kinds of discussions about the construction of female sexuality, about power, the economic basis of relationships, etc., etc.

It soon became apparent that we were a very long way from being able to talk together about such things. Our first stumbling block was the students' resistance to the form of the novel: they lacked the resilience to cope with either the letter format or the dialect. On its own this need not have been a problem for long, but it joined forces, for some of them at least, with a strong desire *not* to become informed about the experience of a viewpoint which might challenge their comfortable white view of events – and, in one or two cases, this was combined with a downright hostility to working on a book by a feminist writer. This never surfaced openly but was expressed in exchanges like this:

> *Me:* Any idea why Alice Walker chose this letter format as a way of telling Celie's story?

> *Boy:* Money? She thought she'd sell more books by something gimmicky?

After this lesson, however, another boy in the group remarked quietly as we were going down the stairs, 'I wouldn't bother about X's reaction you know; he's always going to have problems with a book that has the word "feminist" on the inside cover.'

I wasn't *too* bothered about this individual case of adolescent male chauvinism, but I was keen not to become Alice Walker's apologist in future lessons – a possibility that raised itself the very next day when we were talking about Celie's 'extremist' view of men. 'I mean, it's a bit over the top to write off *all* men the way she does', was how it began. One or two of the girls managed exasperated snorts at this, but inevitably it was me who was left to respond to this 'challenge' in the first instance: 'Er, well . . . have you ever had any contact with anyone who's been through a traumatic experience?' I tried. And then one of the girls joined in. 'You ought to come to the special school I work in. There's a little girl there who's been abused by her father, and she wouldn't even stay in the same room as you, just because you're a man!'

Clearly we had all the circumstances for some heated exchanges and entrenching of positions here – and if the group had been easier with one another, less suspicious, I might have pursued this line further, hoping as always that the other students would supply the alternatives to the reactionary position on Walker as extremist. As it was, I decided to take several paces back and come at the text completely differently.

I was moved in this direction for several reasons: a) two parents complained about it, one only to his daughter, the other by coming to see me, very puzzled as to why his son was having to study a book that was 'mucky' and 'pornographic' (he had read only the first 10 pages); b) discussion of Clause 28 of the Local Government Act 1988, which prohibits the promotion of homosexuality by local authorities, was continually in the news; c) I quite fancied trying to solve one problem (that is, the difficulties relating to content) by tackling what was to me currently a larger and more interesting challenge – how to incorporate ideas from critical theory into our A Level work. And so I set about devising a way of working with the text that would leave difficulties unresolved, rather than seeking to persuade the students that once they 'understood' the novel sufficiently, these issues would be subsumed within their overview of the total text. I lacked the nerve and the skill to embark on a Lacanian analysis of their own subjectivity as readers, so I began rather conventionally by sketching in some information about the development of the novel as a form, mentioning eighteenth-century epistolary novels, and so on. The only 'theory' I attempted was a short discussion of Saussure's de-centring of language and the implications this had for the dominance of realism as a literary form. This the pupils found hard but quite exciting; it was also one of the few lessons I had with them that could be described as enjoyable or 'playful'. All I really wanted at this stage was to question the inevitability of expressive realism, to suggest that writers had many alter-natives available to them, and that during the last decade readers had begun to see the act of reading as a less than straightforward activity. I hoped they might *experience* something of modern critical practice without having to address the theory itself directly. The main ideas I wanted them to appreciate while we worked on *The Color Purple* were:

a) the author is not necessarily the narrator/heroine of the text
b) you are never an innocent reader; you bring a baggage of your own to a text
c) the text is a meeting ground, is problematic, asks questions it doesn't have to answer
d) 'enjoyment' in reading is a complex notion [see 'jouissance' in the glossary – Ed.]
e) meanings are created both in and around a text, rather than contained within it and waiting to be lifted out by the sensitively attuned reader
f) you are more likely to avoid an expressive–realist critical response to a text if you don't share the text's ideology; you can work to produce meaning more effectively if you perceive a distance between yourself and the author.

At this stage I discovered that a colleague in another school had just begun to work on the novel with her Lower VI group. In the interests of 'plurality', this seemed like an opportunity that should not be missed! We agreed that as well as pursuing our own activities each group should communicate by letter or tape with the other group at the beginning and end of this unit of work. We began with a joint letter from Val's group to mine, explaining why they had chosen this particular novel and offering a few first impressions. Joint work not being their forte, my group then wrote back individually, offering a set of first impressions of their own. At the same time we undertook two separate activities. I asked the group to draw up a chart to explain what they found difficult or satisfying about *The Color Purple* and about their previous text, *Twelfth Night*. They worked under the headings of 'problems' and 'rewards', on their own at first and then sharing their reactions with one another. Meanwhile Val's group made a large flow diagram to show the issues and connections both within the book and outside it. These were exchanged along with the letters.

From then on we worked separately again. Every student in each group chose a research area that might illuminate the text and we, with our chartered librarians, supported them in tracking down the less accessible material. Between us we covered the Blues, the Civil Rights movement, biographical work on Alice Walker and her poems. We also researched child sexual abuse. As part of this the group watched a video (borrowed from the NSPCC) of a woman in her thirties talking about her experiences as a child, when she was sexually abused by her father. They did a short piece of writing saying how this account illuminated that particular area in the novel and vice versa. The students were then asked to return to the novel itself, having re-read it, and to undertake one final piece of writing on it. I made it clear to my group that this 'might or might not' be an essay and they jumped at the chance of an 'alternative response'. I received line graphs with commentary, a selection of key passages with explanations of their significance within the whole, key passages from the novel set beside passages from Maya Angelou's *I Know Why the Caged Bird Sings*, with commentary, a diagrammatic representation of the relationships in the novel and an attempt to rewrite certain scenes through the voice of Mr –.

I was only partially happy with these final offerings. It isn't easy to abandon the security of a tried and tested approach and to leap into the unknown. Reading through the work, I had the feeling that I'd only got to first base in the attempt to apply a new critical practice to an A Level text: I'd certainly succeeded in rendering the text problematic and in encouraging students to avoid a subjective overview – but what had they to show for what they'd achieved instead? Or was I just expecting too much too soon? Perhaps it was like tennis lessons, when you've come to that stage where you still can't serve *effectively*, but everyone reassures you by telling you how good it is to be taught systematically so that you will avoid bad habits.

On reflection, I think I would have had an easier time, if I'd just wanted to take the students through some new deconstructive approaches, if I had chosen a text with which they initially felt more comfortable. I still feel, though, that *The Color Purple* was in other ways a good choice, if only because it offered them so little common ground from which to examine relationships.

2   Val Fraser's account

My students showed much less resistance to *The Color Purple* than Gill's students did. I think this was largely because they are a far more cohesive group, and, at the time of choosing the text, they were an all-female group – Paul joined us after Christmas, and just as the reading commenced. I had also introduced some elements of choice. I'd explained that it had to be a text that I felt happy with and one that I felt would interest them, but *The Color Purple* was among four or five texts I introduced to them and asked them to decide upon. They chose *The Color Purple*, I think, because they had heard of the Spielberg film and seen posters of it, and they knew people who had liked the film. Their assumption was that it would be reasonably accessible and not a heavy-weight academic text. They were struggling with D.H. Lawrence's *Sons and Lovers* with their other literature teacher at the time, so this must have influenced their decision, too. As I remember, in their letters to Gill's students they talked about it with glee as having 'lots of blank spaces on each page' and 'sounding like it was a good yarn'.

I was happy with their choice for a number of reasons. Firstly, it was by a woman writer when most of the set texts were by men. So I felt the need to redress the balance of this in their coursework and, indeed, they cited this as a reason too: 'Well, we're doing D.H. Lawrence, so we're getting a lot on what men think.' Also, I wanted them, as a group of young women, to explore a woman's story which raised issues that they would almost certainly face in their futures; for example, the decision to marry, and who to marry, and how relationships with men pervade and even, perhaps, control every woman's life.

I also wanted to introduce them to some positive images of the support women can offer each other in the face of difficult relationships with men. If I could challenge their assumptions that romance conquers all and that other relationships are of less importance, then, I felt, I would have gone some way into getting them to understand that many women feel isolated and forgotten about in marriage in our times.

Finally, I was glad they'd chosen *The Color Purple* because it raised issues that were being aired in the press at the time. Clause 28 of the Local Government Act 1988 and the Cleveland Child Sexual Abuse Enquiry were receiving widespread media coverage. I not only wanted them to discuss these kinds of issues, I wanted them to appreciate that literature is not removed from the culture or context that gave rise to it; that it is not always a means of escaping from the real world. I don't feel as though I'm at odds with Gill here; I'm merely coming to the same conclusion from a different angle. I wanted them to have some realization that the meanings of any text are dependent on what a reader brings to that text, and not only what a writer intends in creating that text. So, if they could understand that a reader in Britain in 1988 experienced a different reaction to reading *The Color Purple* than a reader some five years earlier in another place, then I would be fairly satisfied.

Like Gill, I didn't want them to confuse real events and people with fiction, but I think I was less successful here. I think my group did talk and write as though Celie existed, though Alice Walker didn't help my cause on this point. We read and discussed an article she wrote called 'Writing *The Color Purple*', where she talks about her characters: 'Celie, Shug, Albert, Sofia or Harpo would come for a visit. We would sit wherever I was sitting, and talk. They were always obliging, engaging and jolly.' This view of creating your own world of people really appealed to my students. They would much rather believe that Celie was real than a construction. To this end, it was a good idea they watched the same video that Gill's group did, in which a victim of child sexual abuse recounted her childhood experiences. They found this a lot more raw and frightening.

Lastly, I didn't once use the term 'feminist' to describe the text. This was because I think it is misunderstood and carries with it its own history of prejudice. For young people living in the mining area of North Nottinghamshire, it would have resulted in their feeling alienated from Alice Walker. It would have meant that they approached the text trying to understand her and not themselves, as was really my aim.

Here is what they said about their study of *The Color Purple*:

First impressions

'I was shocked, especially as you'd suggested it.'
'. . . surprised at the way the book was written.'
'I went round showing everybody.'
'I didn't expect to read *that*.'
'It wasn't written down harshly or cruelly or crudely, but you couldn't escape from the nasty bits.'
'I liked the book, but I didn't like what I had to read about.'
'I didn't feel that I could talk about it – it's a taboo subject.' [i.e. sex, lesbianism, child sexual abuse]
'It does challenge your prejudices.'
'It was the first time we'd discussed these issues and had the opportunity to say what we thought, although we'd read about them.'
'We don't talk about these things, and we don't expect literature to, either. It challenges our thinking and what we think is right and wrong.'
'It was my first taste of A Level Lit. and I was a bit worried.'[Paul]
'Crikey! I thought. Have I got to discuss this in class?'
'It wasn't difficult. The writing was strange, but not above us – but it was difficult because it was us that we had to consider.'
'It questions yourself – your thoughts.'

Lasting impressions

'It was useful – you felt you knew Celie as a person as you'd gone through it with her.'
'The ending was disappointing – too sentimental, too tidied-up and complete.'
'I learned a lot about women, especially those who lived at that time and what they had to put up with.'
'It makes you realise it [child sexual abuse] was going on before our time, before Cleveland.'

Is the novel anti-male?

'Yes.'
'Well, no, just anti *that* man, *those* men.'
'It's bound to talk more about, and be critical of, men because it's a female viewpoint and they got so little out of marriage.'

It's worth pointing out that Paul said very little during the lessons and the taping. It must have been difficult for him studying that text and being the only male in the discussions.

Like Gill, I got my group to write letters to the other group, draw diagrams and research topics that interested them from reading the text. However, their major piece of work was an essay and I encouraged them in this. I felt a little anxious, as we hadn't done much traditional response work – we had done diagrammatic representations of Sylvia Plath's poetry, and their own film scripts for *Romeo and Juliet*, so I didn't dare risk any more creatively based tasks, because of the pressures of the examination. By contrast, Gill's group had more experience of straight essays, which they had written for *Klute* and *Twelfth Night*.

Nuggets from their essays

'"You got to fight them, Celie. . . You got to fight them for yourself." This is in my opinion the underlying feeling of all the women in the novel. They are all fighting against men, but in different ways although they want the same right: freedom to be themselves.'

'If Sofia represents the physical force of women, it is Shug who exerts a sexual presence that is as equally powerful in challenging men.'

'It is due greatly, in my opinion, to Shug's sexuality and frankness that Celie is able to be released from her chains. Through their sexual encounters together, Shug is able to show Celie. . . that she has a right to be herself.'

'It was only with enough support from other women, such as the sexual freedom she had gained through Shug and the emotional freedom of realising she had people who supported her, that she had enough power to defeat Mr – and leave.'

'The first feeling that Celie communicates to me is of isolation. The fact that Celie writes to God emphasizes that she has no one else.'

'The only way out of a married woman's misery is to have either female relatives or friends to support you. . . With help from these women Celie was able to break through the isolation she felt.'

Marie's letter to Paul

Dear Paul,

The tasks I have decided to tackle related to *The Color Purple* by Alice Walker are firstly to give a written description explaining the facts and figures on relative themes. I began with physical child abuse as Celie was regularly beaten by her step-father. I went on to emotional abuse because after re-reading *The Color Purple* I realised that both Celie and Nettie are placed under considerable emotional strain, due mainly to the behaviour of the men in the book and therefore emotional abuse becomes important. I then chose to discuss child sexual abuse as this is very apparent in *The Color Purple*. Celie is sexually abused right from the beginning of the book and this surprised me as I did not think this book was going to be so personal. This surprise interested me and that is why I chose sexual abuse. Discovering information was not too difficult as I consulted many text books, newspaper articles and I got in touch with the NSPCC.

I then decided to plot the emotional and physical movements, both upwards and downwards, of Celie, in a diagrammatical form. I did this in the form of a line graph as I thought that this would help me to understand *The Color Purple* and it would also give any reader a sort of summary of parts in the book. I also on the same graph plotted in a different colour the movements of another black girl. This time they are the feelings of Maya Angelou taken from the autobiography *I Know Why The Caged Bird Sings* which I have been reading in my spare time. I chose to accompany my graph with a key as writing on the graph would have been confusing to the reader. I then, as this graph seemed too large to completely analyse, chose a number of points on the graph from *The Color Purple* that I thought were the most crucial events and discussed them. These events included the rape of Celie on page three as this is the first real event in *The Color Purple* and it shows the real despair that Celie is going through. It virtually classes her as a non-person.

I went on to choose seven other points and finally ended with the last paragraph, where Celia and Nettie both feel very young and uplifted by the fact that they are both alive. I then looked at the autobiography by Maya Angelou and tried to find comparisons, which I have discussed, to the eight key points of Celie's life.

I encountered many problems in the reading and studying of *The Color Purple*, the first being a language difficulty. This occurred as *The Color Purple* was written by a black Southern American writer who seems to have a type of 'accent' which made it difficult to read a lot at once and digest it all. This actually became a smaller problem the more I read as I became familiar with Alice Walker's terminology. The next real problem I encountered was the attitude of my parents. They decided that I should not be reading this book. My father's reasons for this decision were that after looking at the contents he thought *The Color Purple* was 'distasteful'. He believed that I should not study this book as the language was unpleasant and the events were the type of events that my father was trying to protect me from. As a family we had a number of discussions about *The Color Purple* and I tried to make my father understand that the acts of rape and child abuse actually did happen in the world about me and that he could not shield me forever. Eventually my father agreed that as the whole of our group were studying the book then it would be unfair to exclude me from the group. This decision did not please my father and this in turn gave me another problem, as I have never wanted to go against my parents' wishes.

After overcoming these problems, I had no other real problems in studying the book until it came to my tasks and then a problem with poetry occurred. I had decided to summarise my thoughts on *The Color Purple* in a poem or a few short verses, but in this task I failed. I knew basically what I wanted to write and what I needed to put but as a poem it just would not work. I eventually got extremely frustrated and decided to use a different approach.

Over all I have gained a lot from reading *The Color Purple* as before I ventured into this kind of book I believed that literature was sort of 'safe'. This was completely different to all my expectations and I realised for the first time that events like rape could actually be written in a book. Literature seemed to be completely new. It became exciting and seemed to give me a different way of looking into horrific ordeals such as rape and child abuse. *The Color Purple* helped me very much as I work at a special school in work experience at college and one of the young girls has been 'raped' by her father and now I understand more about rape and why this particular child dislikes and fears men.

The novel as a whole has led me out into other areas of research. These include reading *I Know Why The Caged Bird Sings*, the autobiography by Maya Angelou, some essays by Alice Walker including 'Saving the life that is your own' and 'The Civil Rights movement: What good was it?' It also led me to reading Maya Angelou's poetry and a book called *Dibs* by V. Axline, which enabled me to write about emotional child abuse. All of these sources of information I have enjoyed and would recommend to all, but *The Color Purple* was for me the most moving and fulfilling. It opened many doors to new and overwhelming experience.

The Color Purple was a very inspiring book and I hope that I get a chance to read other books of this type as it was a rewarding experience that dealt with events I did not really relate to. Now I understand how widespread rape, incest and child victimisation are and just how drastic the effects can be.

Thank you for your correspondence on the novel *The Color Purple* and related work. Hope that the rest of your course goes well and that everyone in your group receives the grade that they deserve. If you cover any other topics and want to discuss them, then just write. I will help if it is possible.

Goodbye for now,

Marie

8 Working with *Wuthering Heights* and *Persuasion* at A Level

Steve Bennison and Jim Porteous

Steve Bennison now teaches English and Communications in a Bristol technical college, having previously worked for ten years in comprehensive schools. An active member of the Avon branch of NATE, he is currently involved in work on a proposed 'Literary and Cultural Studies' A Level.

Jim Porteous is Head of English and Communication Studies at a Bristol comprehensive school. He has been involved in the setting up and running of a county-wide Mode 3 GCSE English and English Literature consortium and has written articles with Steve Bennison about, in particular, autobiography and detective fiction, theoretically based approaches to classic texts, and the Victorian novelist 'Mark Rutherford'.

This chapter describes two brief episodes in a two-year A Level Literature course, a study of Emily Brontë's *Wuthering Heights* during the first term and a later analysis of Jane Austen's *Persuasion*. These reflect a practice developed over several years' experience of teaching the coursework component of the AEB 660 syllabus, and bear the scars of frustrations inherent in the way in which the 660 exam papers expect innocently responsive readings of single texts and implicitly discourage any theoretical, historical or political considerations, a 'philosophy' which often tends to spill over into the coursework element too, despite its nominal openness.[1]

The teaching described here is, therefore, to some extent 'against the grain', in that its primary aim is to encourage an active understanding of ideology and discourse and the ways these are produced and reproduced within literature and criticism. We see this work less as a theoretical approach to a text than as a textual approach to a theory – and the 'theory' here as a political tool rather than simply an episode in the history of literary criticism. There is a difference, however, between the teacher's aims and what students themselves actually experience, understand and apply, and we have tried to concentrate in this account particularly on the relatively mundane processes of conventional 'progressive' classroom activity – reading, discussion, groupwork, writing of various kinds, etc. – and on what we would hope students would learn from these.

> Can the measure of that passionate intensity truly be taken by the blundering techniques of some literary sociology? Do we not find in that sense of an ultimate bedrock of being which haunts Catherine Earnshaw a supreme instance of great art's resistance to a merely sociological reading?[2]

> Where, it will be objected, are the conditions of nineteenth century capitalism in such a purely 'prophetic' novel as *Wuthering Heights*? Surely no materialist view could explain this book? What relation has it to the nineteenth century? It is beyond time and space, immortal, primeval and elementary as the passion which gives the book its life. It is the novel become pure poetry.[3]

Well, yes, *Wuthering Heights* is indeed crucially bound up with the conditions of nineteenth-century capitalism and, by analysing this, a materialist 'literary sociology' can explain both the interesting notion of 'an ultimate bedrock of being' and the critical discourses which reproduce the text in these elaborately hyperbolic and deeply ideological terms. *Wuthering Heights* is, in fact, in many ways an ideal text with which to begin such work, concerned centrally with the relation between 'ultimate bedrocks of being' and class and gender, power and oppression, and exploring these in an extraordinarily 'open', experimental form, in which the ideological determinants of representation and interpretation, of reading and writing, are foregrounded and made available for analysis and discussion.

Beginning their reading of *Wuthering Heights*, the students found themselves in the company of another reader, Lockwood. Lockwood is, however, a patently incompetent reader and, having read the first two chapters, it was a useful and amusing introductory exercise to list his various howlers and misinterpretations: mistaking Hareton for a servant, Cathy for Heathcliff's wife, and complimenting her on her favourite pets only to discover that they are a brace of dead rabbits, and so on. Critics' readings of the novel, of course, frequently begin with this point, and it has become conventional to see Lockwood as in some way representative of the reader:

> Lockwood's response is more or less what the response of the ordinary reader might be expected to be . . . Lockwood here is a kind of surrogate reader . . . Lockwood, the reader's vicarious representative in the novel . . .[4]

Such assumptions of a single, universal reader, constructed apparently by the text itself, neglect, however, that Lockwood is very clearly the product of a specific class and gender formation. A brief discussion of his misreadings revealed that almost all have a social origin and, although also themselves new arrivals in relation to the text, the students were quick to point out that the man is a male, bourgeois twit, and likely, therefore, to read along somewhat different lines from their own. Implicitly, they had begun to recognize the concept of differential readings, the way that meaning is always produced partly by the ideological position that readers bring to texts. This is scarcely a revolutionary point, but it is often a new and liberating idea for A Level students – and one often denied by AEB 660 exam questions, with their insistent intentionalist assumption that 'the author' produces 'effects' in 'us'.

Asked next to read chapter 3, the group then traced Lockwood's attempts to read and respond to the situation he finds himself in at the Heights, building up a diagram to represent this:[5]

LOCKWOOD	WUTHERING HEIGHTS
Bourgeois city dandy, man-nered, emotionally repressed (e.g. previous romance), expects others to agree to suit him, conventional – tries to interpret WH in orderly terms (e.g. family relations), consensus and moderation.	Wild, 'natural' energy and emotion (e.g. previous romance), internal conflict, repels intruders, disordered defiance of conventional norms (e.g. family relations), conflict and extremes.

→ Breaks into WH, trespassing despite warnings and rejection, penetrates locked room, within banned room, within locked WH, unlock-(wood)ing things normally kept firmly lock(wood)ed

→ Orgasmic fantasising about the Catherines, coming near to the heart of the WH story

→ Reading the illicit, rebellious marginalia instead of the orthodox moral text – i.e. reading a text within a text within a text within a text

→ Dreams about interrupting and rebelling against strict moral religious sermon on orthodox biblical text

→ Dreams of tree tapping – tapping his subconscious – smashes the window

→ Grabbed by icy hand – comes into physical contact with the WH story, passion, desperation

← Too much! Severs the contact, cuts himself off, lock(wood)s it out

← Blocks the hole with pile of books

← Scurries home to Nelly. Gets her to tell him a safe, defused, bedtime-story version of WH

By this stage, it was becoming apparent that we have here a book all about reading and writing, competing kinds of interpretation and expression, and that these were not simply a matter of individual points of view and personal response, but in fact the site of a grim life-and-death struggle for power and control. Even if the precise nature of this power and control was not yet clear, the students were able to recognize the interaction of class and gender, sexuality and self, oppression and rebellion.

At this point, however, Lockwood retires to the Grange and employs Nelly as a replacement reader and interpreter. Having read a few chapters of Nelly's narration, most A Level students will find it considerably more attractive than Lockwood's: in contrast to his arrogantly pompous, convoluted style, Nelly's language is seductively reassuring and recognizable in its down-to-earth common sense. To encourage a questioning and problematizing of this response, the students were presented with a selection of brief extracts from critics' comments describing Nelly's 'personality' and function in the novel:

> She represents the maximum objectivity possible. The key words 'think, reflective faculties, steady, reasonable, sharp discipline, wisdom' emphasise the essential normality, the spiritual poise which informs the novel. And it is important that her wisdom is not exclusively a rural heritage; it is also derived from wide reading, and it is this which endows her with a width and generosity of opinion.[6]
>
> To take Nelly Dean as 'benevolent' and 'wholesomely nurturing', and 'detached' from the story she tells, is to take for granted the very assumptions on which she works in order to 'cook' the narrative and render herself invisible, and it is to miss some of the more complex and disturbing implications of her situation.[7]
>
> Nelly Dean seems to have incurred a good deal of unjustified ill-will and perverse misrepresentation. We identify with Nelly Dean, with her wholesome classlessness and her spontaneous maternal impulses. She is most carefully, consistently and convincingly created for us as the normal woman, whose truly feminine nature satisfies itself in nurturing all the children in the book.[8]
>
> Patriarchy's housekeeper, charged with policing the realm she represents.[9]
>
> She is like someone confidently approaching the sea with a mop.[10]
>
> Let us abandon the comfortable conception of 'Nelly', and analyse instead the signs and units of language which constitute 'her'.[11]

Discussion of a selection of extracts like these was given a small twist of additional sophistication, and amusement, by getting students to write Nelly's own reactions and responses to these descriptions. This gradually revealed the way in which Nelly's apparently unified, authoritative 'personality', her resolute, dependable consistency, is in fact riddled with internal splits, gaps and contradictions. Rather than representing a single 'point of view', she is perhaps best seen as a walking battleground of conflicting discourses, further complicated by her ambiguous position as a character in her own narration. This was demonstrated by asking the group to find in the text illustrations of, for example, Nelly as servant/matriarch; worker/snob; rebel/conformist; agent of fantasy/repression; and by looking at the tensions in particular passages of her narration between apparently unmediated mimetic reporting and 'unreliable' diegetic fabrication. A reconsideration, at this stage, of the selection of criticism reinforced the point that criticism, too, is a battleground of conflicting readings, privileging and celebrating some aspects while censuring, marginalizing or silencing others in order to produce a single authoritative reading which supports particular interests and values.

By the time the group had read to the end of the first part of the book, they were in a position to deal explicitly with the notion of discourse. This was begun at the formal level of textual discourse, building on the deconstruction of Nelly and referring to other novels that the students had read.

What Kind of Text is *Wuthering Heights?*

Classic realist texts: this is a term used to describe most novels written in the nineteenth century – it describes those novels in which there is one obvious dominant and controlling 'voice'. This voice, which is usually the author's, though it can belong to a character in the novel who represents what the author 'stands for' and wants to say, puts all the other characters and events in the novel into perspective: it makes clear, for example, who are the 'good' and who the 'bad' characters; it tells us, in effect, how to judge and read what's going on. This main voice is called the *privileged discourse*: discourse, because it is like a controlling and selective voice; privileged because it is not open to question – you may not agree with it and you can criticize it, but in the novel it is not open to question or negotiation.

How does this apply to *Wuthering Heights*? Is it a classic realist text? We have already noticed that there are actually quite a lot of other texts (books, sermons, diaries, letters, etc.) within the one main text, so any privileged discourse is going to have to compete with all these to start with.

Secondly, and more significantly, Lockwood and Nelly Dean both assume that their voice, the discourse that they share, is privileged, that it is not open to any challenges or questions. What they say and write is, in their opinion, exactly what the reader is meant to read and agree with. *But* we have seen that Lockwood's discourse is highly suspect and untrustworthy (mainly due to his class, perhaps). And if Lockwood's discourse is not privileged, is Nelly Dean's any the more so?

To answer this, we have to look at how she controls the story she tells: what language does she use; what comments does she make on the actions and the characters; what part does she actually play in the story; most importantly, has she actually understood all that is going on – can she, or does she even want to, comprehend all the strange and passionate experiences that make up the lives of the characters she is involved with and whose story she tries to tell?

If you agree with her and Lockwood that her discourse is beyond question, then you will read the novel as a classic realist text. If, on the other hand, you can find sufficient evidence within the text and the story she tells to put her own telling of the story in doubt, then you will read the novel in a different way – it will be an *interrogative text*. In an interrogative text there is no single privileged discourse, *even though* there may appear to be so and some characters lay claim to it. Their discourse becomes one of many, all competing for prominence, none of which emerge as the 'final word' on the subject.

Most students were able to grasp the distinction between classic realist and interrogative text. *Wuthering Heights* was generally considered, however, a problematic case, somehow occupying both positions simultaneously. Discussion of this point led to an important extension of the original formal dualism, recognizing that what is involved is not simply inherent properties of the text itself but also the question of how it is read. This has in fact been conceded by Catherine Belsey, whose *Critical Practice*[12] was probably most responsible for popularizing the original distinction:

> It now seems to me that this classification may have been excessively formalistic, implying that texts can unilaterally determine their reception by the reader. As we now know, a reading practice which actively seeks out contradiction can *produce* as interrogative a text which has conventionally been read as declarative.[13]

A second, even more important, extension, however, is to recognize that the discourses at work in the writing and reading of any text are not simply a 'literary' matter, but the product of ideological forces at work in their society generally, inextricably if complicatedly bound up with the social discourses in which wider ideological conflicts are fought out. Analysis of a text in these terms inevitably means an analysis of ideology:

> Bourgeois ideology presents itself, or imposes itself in our consciousness, as a totality, as an extremely well-constructed, coherent system. . . Ideology produces an effect of coherence, but does that mean it is? Not at all. On the contrary, ideology is essentially contradictory, riddled with all sorts of conflicts which it attempts to conceal. All kinds of devices are constructed in order to conceal these contradictions; but by concealing them, they somehow reveal them. The type of analysis which I propose is precisely to read the ideological contradictions within the devices produced to conceal them, to reconstitute the contradictions from their system of concealment.[14]

Perhaps the most important, and certainly the most immediate, issue arising from considering *Wuthering Heights* in these terms is the sense, attested by generations of critics, study aids and exam questions, that the story somehow involves matters of 'universal', 'timeless' relevance and significance. Discussion of this idea produced a list of such topics – childhood, the family, love, death, nature, wild/civilized, material/spiritual, heaven/hell, good/evil – and the students were then asked to collect brief examples from the text dealing with each. From the evidence thus assembled, however, it quickly became apparent that, far from being rooted in timeless certainties, even within the book these supposed 'universals' appeared in a bewildering variety of different, often contradictory, forms, their meaning and significance produced by the range of conflicting discourses from which the book is constructed – despite Nelly's attempts to harness them all to a single, authoritative reading. Discussing this idea in her introduction to a recent edition of the novel, Heather Glen argues that,

Emily Brontë is indeed concerned with that in human experience which seems to be universal and unchanging. But it appears in her novel through the prism of a whole constellation of quite specific early Victorian discourses, each of which carries its own distinct and distinctive reasonances, implications, and senses of possibility... Certainly, in *Wuthering Heights* they intertwine in complex ways: they cannot be separated, or simply attributed to different characters. Yet, equally, they cannot be seen as blending, unproblematically, into a harmonious, univocal vision. Indeed, much of the disturbing life of the novel comes from the tensions and contradictions between them.[15]

It is difficult to deal with this with any adequacy at A Level. Traditional teaching, of course, simply relegates the whole question to the marginal status of a 'background', requiring only a cursory consideration before getting on with the business of studying 'the text itself'. Despite its nominal openness to all 'approaches', such traditions often survive within AEB 660, reinforced by the way in which the coursework requirements and weighting of marks are built on the assumption that the standard pattern will be to spend three or four weeks each studying a series of single texts. Nevertheless, even within these constraints, it was possible for the group to work briefly on a selection of extracts from contemporary writing, exemplifying early nineteenth-century religious, Romantic and political discourse:

For my part, I call education . . . that which tends to consolidate a firm and regular system of character; that which tends to form a friend, a companion, and a wife . . . that which inculcates principles, polishes taste, regulates temper, cultivates reason, subdues the passions, directs the feelings, habituates to reflection, trains to self-denial, and, more especially, that which refers all actions, feelings, sentiments, tastes and passions to the love and fear of God.[16]

Heaven and Hell seem to be placed in view of each other . . . by this means the happiness of the Saints in Heaven is immensely enlarged . . . And on the other side: the misery of the damned in Hell is no less increased. For the anguish of that fire and brimstone in which they are weltering is greatly aggravated by a sight of those glories which they have irrecoverably and eternally lost.[17]

The road of excess leads to the palace of wisdom . . . He who desires but acts not, breeds pestilence . . . Prisons are built with stones of law, brothels with bricks of religion . . . The tygers of wrath are wiser than the horses of instruction.[18]

When a tract is left me (which is the case almost every Sunday) I examine it, and where I find a blank, there I write some very pithy political or philosophical sentence, and so make them subservient to a purpose diametrically opposed to their intent – namely, the diffusion of truth.[19]

By examining a selection of extracts like these, tracing the parallels and contradictions in their discursive strategies and relating these to the strategies employed in the novel, the students were able to begin to develop some sense of contemporary ideological forms, and to see the novel as reflecting, orchestrating and contributing to the continuing conflict between them. Approaching the novel in this way allowed the students to see it as intimately and inseparably related to its historical, political conditions of production, without limiting this to a reductionist one-for-one 'symbolism'. So, yes, Heathcliff could simultaneously 'represent' both the oppressed proletariat and emergent forms of capitalism, if by this we mean that the discursive strategies which construct Heathcliff as a character bear significant similarities to the discourses in which early nineteenth-century political conflicts were expressed and understood. Certainly, whatever its validity in pure theoretical terms, this approach provided a useful illustration of the invisible way in which ideology works, through language and institutions, pervading all social discourse. It also proved a pragmatically valuable enabling strategy in the classroom, allowing students to draw on their own reading, their observations, insights and understanding, and make sense of these within a broad critical and political framework, incorporating them into a totalizing overview when appropriate but without feeling pressured to do so prematurely. It provided a technique which the class subsequently went on to apply to other texts ranging from Dickens' *Hard Times* to Shakespeare's *The Tempest*.

Having thus spent some time examining the construction of the first half of the novel, the students were now able to deal with the second half rather more summarily. Again, discussion was provoked and directed by considering a selection of criticism. Possible readings of the second half of the novel were soon recognized as falling into two fairly distinct categories. In the first category were those readings which presented the second half as natural, healthy and artistically satisfying; a reconciliation, ordering and transcendence of the conflicting elements of the first half; a steady progress towards maturity:

> The natural cycle of the seasons will bring renewal; spring follows winter; there is birth as well as death. The second half of the novel shows us this force at work. The whole story is told a second time, in reverse, until a balance is achieved, a vision of cosmic totality embracing the forces of nature, beautiful but fierce, with moral and existential choice in human beings. The truth embodied within that vision is really a very simple one, like, I suspect, all great truths.[20]
>
> *Wuthering Heights* is not an unpleasant novel. It is in fact a very precisely balanced structure of pleasant and unpleasant, normal and abnormal. It relegates all the potentially unhealthy elements to their place in the artistic whole, and moves continually towards a reflection of perfect tranquillity.[21]
>
> Nelly Dean's adult and selflessly maternal behaviour prepares us for the evolution of Catherine. With similar drives and temptations to her mother's, she is able to profit by experience and get a moral education from

> her sufferings. We see her transcend the psychological temptations and impulses which would have made her repeat her mother's history; and this is not a question of sociology or social history but is timeless. Catherine is clearly offered as something ponderable about the nature of the human family in general and an assertion of the novelist's belief in free-will.[22]

Predictably enough, in the light of their previous work, the group viewed this kind of reading with deep suspicion. It was seen as smoothing over and effacing conflicts which still remained unresolved; and, although this is certainly Nelly's project throughout the second half of the novel, her narration never entirely succeeds in coming to terms with all its recalcitrant material.

> The second half of the text constructs complex bonds between all the characters to intensify the exclusion of Heathcliff as other. It is a terribly frenetic construction of family ties, distancing the threat of the non-familial, the unfamiliar. The family excludes anything foreign to itself as being unnatural. It guarantees stability through limitation and closure. By the end the threat represented by Heathcliff and Cathy has been exorcised by confining it to their own vampiric relationship; they are mere restless spirits drifting around the abandoned enclosure of the Heights.[23]

An alternative way of reading the second half, therefore, was to recognize and analyse this process of smoothing over, and to retrieve the ideological forces thus effaced and excluded. In this way, the second half of the novel was seen as a continuation of the conflicts of the first, presented this time not as tragedy but as farce, in a determined attempt to achieve what Pierre Macherey calls 'the fictional resolution of ideological contradictions.'[24]

Examining specific passages in the light of this, the students were now able to see a complex irony in the scenes in which Hareton is taught to read:

> 'Con-*trary!*' said a voice, as sweet as a silver bell – 'That for the third time, you dunce! I'm not going to tell you again – Recollect, or I pull your hair!'
> 'Contrary, then,' answered another, in deep, but softened tones. 'And now, kiss me, for minding so well.'
> 'No, read it over first correctly, without a single mistake.'
> . . . I overheard no further distinguishable talk; but on looking round again, I perceived two such radiant countenances bent over the page of the accepted book, that I did not doubt the treaty had been ratified, on both sides, and the enemies were, thenceforth, sworn allies. The work they studied was full of costly pictures; and these, and their position, had charm enough to keep them unmoved . . .[25]

Presided over by Lockwood and Nelly, the establishment of 'the accepted book' here serves almost as a symbolic reference to the function of the repetitive second half of the novel, and to the discourses of 'education' generally, in ensuring ideological adaptation to shifts in economic and political power. As David Musselwhite points out, 'The very function of the literary is to accommodate and conciliate that "contrary".'[26] At the risk of sounding glib, the 'accepted book' episode is a salutary reminder, in fact, that all reading is a political act, and that the teaching and criticism supporting it are political too.

It was with some relief, then, that the group finally read the last pages of the novel, where, despite the apparent success of this newly established hegemony, we are still left with the spectral reminder of an oppositional alternative and, despite Lockwood's nervous assurances, surely the promise of continuing conflict.

Persuasion was the last text studied as part of the AEB 660 coursework requirements, in a three-week period towards the end of the final spring term. The work on the novel outlined below was an attempt to bring together and apply a number of the ideas and approaches first introduced in the study of *Wuthering Heights* and which had since then been elaborated and added to over the duration of the course. Again, the approach employed in the classroom did not specifically refer to named theorists or critical methodologies, although an earlier unit of work on autobiography had set up a nodding acquaintance with the outlines of psychoanalysis, via a selection of passages from Freud's *The Interpretation of Dreams* and the *Introductory Lectures:* some of this knowledge, especially that relating to the notion of repression, was called upon and developed during the course of the analysis of Austen's troubled text.

One of the declared objectives which the students shared was to locate and explain the ways in which *Persuasion*, honoured as a model of the closed text (a 'dramatic and spiritual unity' according to David Cecil),[27] with its attention to the strictest of unities in terms of characterization, locations and dates, for instance, was in fact, precisely because of its concentration on achieving and maintaining a sense of order, the site of all manner of unwelcome disturbances, revealing silences and striking contradictions. This approach made it possible to take up a manifestly reactionary novel (in political terms) and re-read it in a radical way (a very minor contribution to the history of the novel's reproduction). *Persuasion* was chosen, then, partly because it offered the students the chance to engage in a critical and challenging course of study and to apply and extend previous approaches. It was also, given the time available, conveniently short, and the group had read and studied *Emma* as an examination set text, thus allowing for a lot of fruitful cross-referencing (and handy revision). The central theoretical basis for the work, which helped determine the choice of text and the nature of the study, is contained in the following comments by Pierre Macherey:

> Literary works appear 'healthy', almost perfect, so that all one can do is accept them and admire them. But in fact their reality does not accord with their self-presentation. Personally, texts please me, I find them beautiful **not because they are 'healthy' but because they are sick, because within them they express the contradictions of the social reality in which they are produced.** [28]

In this light it seemed worth examining whether Austen's novel, thoroughly appropriated along with her other works by a bourgeois ideology, might not reveal itself as a text suffering from some chronic complaints.

The group began by reading the opening four chapters for themselves; the first lesson was spent outlining and clarifying the various family relationships, the range of characters and their dealings with one another, the topography, the history, and in predicting what might be expected to ensue. (The session was livened up when one student recited Sir Walter's disquisition upon the evils of a nautical life.)[29] The group noted Austen's closely detailed presentation of 'real' places and characters and contrasted this with the unsettling consequences of Sir Walter's inattention to detail and other people. A few of the main points concerning 'people and places' were then summarized on a sheet showing family trees, dates, and so on. (See diagram 1.)

Over the next week the students finished reading the novel, during which time the work in class concentrated on two main areas: the hierarchy of discourses, and the roles available to women within the text. The privileged discourse, clearly, is that of the author, possessing a wealth of knowledge about the characters' personalities, motivation and thoughts as well as judging by comment and implication. The apparently controlling discourse, within the social hierarchy that's set up, is Sir Walter's; surrounded by mirrors, he is self-defining, (well-) regarded by those whose services he buys (Mr Shepherd) and by those who desire his favours (Mrs Clay). In this sense he is impervious to Austen's withering criticisms and to the complaints of those he chooses to ignore: 'The party drove off in very good spirits; Sir Walter prepared with condescending bows for all the afflicted tenantry and cottagers who might have had a hint to shew themselves' (p. 63). Her father and elder sister, blinded by their vanity and self-seeking, pay no attention to Anne. She is unheeded and is presented only to us as she 'really' is, with her discourse validated by the privileged discourse whose values she shares: 'but Anne, with an elegance of mind and a sweetness of character, which must have placed her high with any people of real understanding, was nobody with either father or sister: her word had no weight; her convenience was always to give way; – she was only Anne' (p. 37). The group noted the challenge to prove themselves readers of 'real understanding', in Austen's terms, and to accept the ideological values of the privileged discourse.

The students also considered the striking contrasts between the lives of leisure enjoyed by the men and women of the landed gentry and their respective expectations. The means by which these social roles are constructed and confirmed is reflected, for example, in the following passage: 'Immediately surrounding Mrs Musgrove were the little Harvilles, whom she was sedulously guarding from the tyranny of the two children from the Cottage, expressly arrived to amuse them. On one side was a table, occupied by some chattering girls, cutting up silk and gold paper; and on the other were tressels and trays, bending under the weight of brawn and cold pies, where riotous boys were holding high revel' (p. 148). A list drawn up to

DIAGRAM I **People and Places**

The story begins in the summer of 1814: the first four chapters fill in the marital and non-marital histories of the three Elliot daughters:
– Elizabeth's expected marriage to William Elliot, heir to the Elliot estates, came to nothing (he met her once and, despite invitations to the Hall, never saw her again)
– Anne was persuaded to 'refuse' Frederick Wentworth
– Mary is married

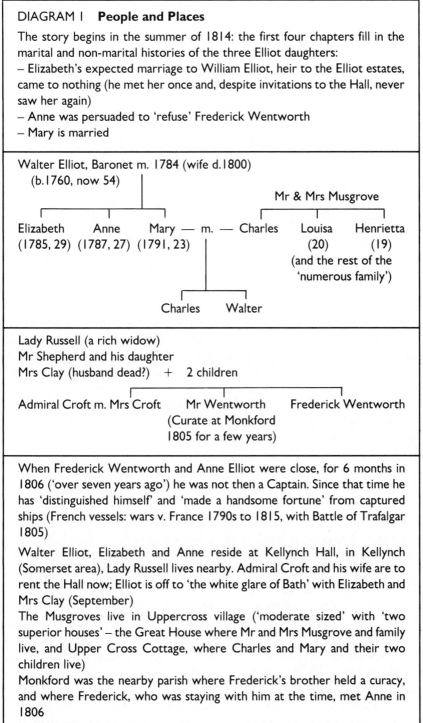

Walter Elliot, Baronet m. 1784 (wife d.1800)
(b.1760, now 54)

Mr & Mrs Musgrove

Elizabeth   Anne   Mary — m. — Charles   Louisa   Henrietta
(1785, 29) (1787, 27) (1791, 23)   (20)   (19)
                                                    (and the rest of the
                                                    'numerous family')

Charles   Walter

Lady Russell (a rich widow)
Mr Shepherd and his daughter
Mrs Clay (husband dead?)   +   2 children

Admiral Croft m. Mrs Croft   Mr Wentworth   Frederick Wentworth
                              (Curate at Monkford
                              1805 for a few years)

When Frederick Wentworth and Anne Elliot were close, for 6 months in 1806 ('over seven years ago') he was not then a Captain. Since that time he has 'distinguished himself' and 'made a handsome fortune' from captured ships (French vessels: wars v. France 1790s to 1815, with Battle of Trafalgar 1805)

Walter Elliot, Elizabeth and Anne reside at Kellynch Hall, in Kellynch (Somerset area), Lady Russell lives nearby. Admiral Croft and his wife are to rent the Hall now; Elliot is off to 'the white glare of Bath' with Elizabeth and Mrs Clay (September)

The Musgroves live in Uppercross village ('moderate sized' with 'two superior houses' – the Great House where Mr and Mrs Musgrove and family live, and Upper Cross Cottage, where Charles and Mary and their two children live)

Monkford was the nearby parish where Frederick's brother held a curacy, and where Frederick, who was staying with him at the time, met Anne in 1806

In 1809 Charles Musgrove could not persuade Anne to marry him, so he married Mary instead record instances of men revelling in their country pleasures (Charles Musgrove, for instance; see also p. 70) or seeking glory on the high seas contrasted with the empty, passive nature of the women's experiences: 'Such were Elizabeth Elliot's sentiments and sensations; such the cares to alloy, the agitations to vary, the sameness and the elegance, the prosperity and the nothingness, of her scene of life – such the feelings to give interest to a long, uneventful residence in one country circle, to fill the vacancies which there were no habits of utility abroad, no talents or accomplishments for home, to occupy' (p. 40). Their lives are subordinated to, and determined by, the 'tyranny' of men: the women count themselves, and are seen as, failures if they lack a husband (Elizabeth); they are suspected of baseness and deviousness if they try to find one for themselves (Mrs Clay); their lives are almost unrelentingly dire once they are married (Lady Elliot, Mrs Smith and, most notably, Mary). Another list produced by the group recorded the types of activities the women were expected to practise (e.g. 'the females were fully occupied in all the other subjects of house-keeping, neighbours, dress, dancing, and music', p. 69).

Only a naval husband, it appeared, could be depended upon to negate successfully the 'nothingness' of woman's 'scene of life' (the Crofts and the Harvilles). This qualification became increasingly significant over the next two weeks, and was kept in mind when the students now addressed themselves to a new question: given that the text reflects social institutions – the family, marriage, and so on – that construct and oppress women to an appalling extent, could the text be read as a conscious, intended criticism of these social formations, or were these taken for granted, as acceptable? As the students commented, it seemed obvious that the Elliot daughters, for example, were severely repressed and each one of them sick. Elizabeth's 'answer' was to adopt a public haughtiness and attach herself to her grotesque father, whilst Mary was suffering from terminal neurotic symptoms, constantly ill, demanding and repelling possible sources of comfort. Anne, too, the students were quick to point out, was prone to disturbing, disordered sensations. With some surprise the group, after wrangling and argument, arrived at the inescapable conclusion that, far from offering a deliberated and devastating radical critique of the way these particular women of the landed gentry were constructed within the existing social formations, the text was either presenting stunningly reactionary solutions or, as in most cases, was not even acknowledging any problem. But that, of course, doesn't prevent it revealing the grounds for a necessary radical critique – of the lives the women are forced to lead, and of the novel itself. (The example of Louisa neatly encapsulates the values of the privileged discourse: rather too immature and flighty, she makes one rash leap too many; in falling she is battered into some sort of submissive order and is now ready for a quiet life as an attentive wife to the dolorous Captain Benwick.)

It was recognized, then, that the novel was in fact working to resist change; those whose warped natures (William Elliot, Mrs Clay) or whose vanity and incompetence (Sir Walter) threatened to bring about disorder (in the context of acceptable marriages, the upkeep of the landed tradition, and so on) are those Austen attacks most fiercely. The most desirable state (though, appearances being the troublesome things they are, this will not become apparent until virtue is properly recognized and rewarded at the close of the tale) is one that actively seeks to resist change and to preserve and confirm the old social order. Before analysing the significance of the Navy in this respect, the group first reconsidered the position of Anne and the reasons why she, initially unheeded by others, should be so celebrated by the privileged discourse. As the students had commented before, unlike Emma (who starts out heeded by all but badly in need of some of the mature wisdom that comes from a series of chastening yet educative experiences), Anne is held up from the word go as an example of achieved maturity and balanced perfection. That others do not immediately recognize this indicates their sorry lack of real understanding (Wentworth's task in the novel is to refamiliarize himself with Anne's considerable virtues and loyalty; throughout the novel Anne makes only one error, when she believes for a time that Wentworth seeks to avoid her (p. 84)). Anne's essential quality is that she does not have to change; her role is to recover and reassert the past, in terms of her relationship with Wentworth, and on a reactionary, ideological level too. To help sort out and confirm their own reading at this stage the group was given a sheet presenting categories into which Austen's characters fall, using an outline devised by Terry Lovell [30] and spent a lesson deciding where characters from *Persuasion* and *Emma* should be placed (for their results, see diagram 2).

It now became possible to start working out some possible reasons for the odd disturbances that Anne seemed particularly prone to, and to relate these instances of disorder to the repression under which she labours, and which the text cannot wholly conceal. Another spell of hunting down examples produced a surprisingly lengthy and revealing list of occasions when the finely ordered Anne was shaken into a severe state of agitation by the physical presence and touch of Captain Wentworth. One of the first of the 'agitation episodes' (p. 103) has been commented on before, by Professor Morris Zapp in his seminar on 'Eros and Agape in the later novels of Jane Austen':

> Getting into his stride, Morris demonstrated that Mr Elton was obviously impotent because there was no lead in the pencil that Harriet Smith took from him; and the moment in *Persuasion* when Captain Wentworth lifted the little brat Walter off Anne Elliot's shoulders . . . He snatched up the book and read with feeling:' " . . .she found herself in the state of being released from him . . . Before she realised that Captain Wentworth had done it . . . he was resolutely borne away . . . Her sensations on the discovery made her perfectly speechless. She could not even thank him. She could only hang over little Charles with the most disordered feelings." How about that?' he concluded reverently. 'If that isn't an orgasm, what is it?'[31]

Zapp's students look flabbergasted, but perhaps they are responding to the man's impromptu display as much as to what he has said. Professor Zapp's

DIAGRAM 2   **Categories of Austen Characters**

Maximum possible good which *may* be achieved within each category indicated by capitals.

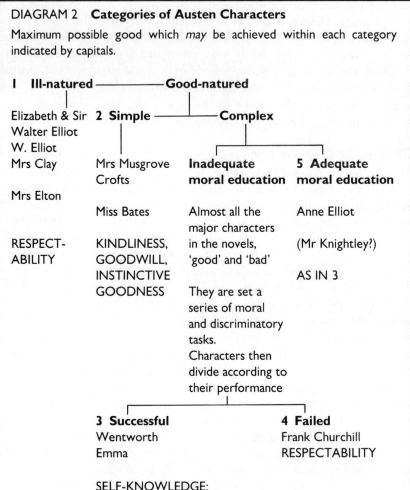

1 Ill-natured ——————Good-natured

Elizabeth & Sir   **2 Simple ————┴————Complex**
Walter Elliot
W. Elliot
Mrs Clay   Mrs Musgrove   **Inadequate   5 Adequate**
                      Crofts   **moral education   moral education**
Mrs Elton

                      Miss Bates   Almost all the   Anne Elliot
                                        major characters
RESPECT-   KINDLINESS,   in the novels,   (Mr Knightley?)
ABILITY   GOODWILL,   'good' and 'bad'
                      INSTINCTIVE   AS IN 3
                      GOODNESS   They are set a
                                        series of moral
                                        and discriminatory
                                        tasks.
                                        Characters then
                                        divide according to
                                        their performance

                      3 Successful   **4 Failed**
                      Wentworth   Frank Churchill
                      Emma   RESPECTABILITY

                      SELF-KNOWLEDGE:
                      ACTIONS AND RELATIONSHIPS
                      DETERMINED BY MORAL AND
                      RELIGIOUS PRINCIPLES

The categories don't fit all characters neatly – Jane Fairfax hovers between 3 and 4, for example

As we've seen, Anne doesn't need to change (which is probably why she gets so agitated . . .)

Even in *Emma*, however, though the character of Emma does 'change', there's no question of pointing out that the social order needs changing. *Emma* combines order and energy/libido at crucial moments in dances – order and movement in a well-established pattern. Perhaps the fact that Emma marries a substitute father-figure stresses the extent to which the text is against social change and in favour of characters learning to 'fit in' to a predetermined and apparently established social order – and the price paid for this repression.

somewhat laboured example could have been easily replaced by a number of others: 'Still, however, she had enough to feel! It was agitation, pain, pleasure, a something between delight and misery' (p. 185). The point that was established within the A Level group was not that *Persuasion* might unwittingly describe a succession of orgasms, nor that this is what Anne 'really' wants. What is significant is not so much the type of experience described (which is undoubtedly sexual in nature) but the eager, strained force of the language and the feelings Anne experiences, in complete contrast to her apparently secure and ordered 'essential' self. Of course, meeting and coming into close contact with a man she has loved and for whom she still cares will be expected to affect her; it is the extent of the agitation and the increasing violence of the disturbances that is important. The students were able to suggest that the force of her emotions at these moments acts as a kind of register to record the extent to which, in her everyday life, she is repressed. (Another example of the force of repression arises when Wentworth and Anne have to correspond by letter even when pressed together in the same room.) Taking this further, a line of argument was developed to tie these instances of a revealed repression with the point about Anne's not needing to change: again, are the sources of repression to be overcome by a form of radical social change, or does Austen offer another solution?

In the final week of their study of the novel, the group set about considering the significance of the Navy in the text. The naval types had already been noted as being especially honoured by the privileged discourse and because of their fine record on the marital front. Anne herself praised the men of the English task force early in the novel: 'The navy, I think, who have done so much for us, have at least an equal claim with any other set of men, for all the comforts and all the privileges which any home can give' (p. 49). The Navy which has 'done so much for us' still has one crucial role to play now the wars are over. Its economic and ideological function is referred to when Anne later considers the role played by the Crofts at Kellynch Hall: 'she had in fact so high an opinion of the Crofts, and considered her father so very fortunate in his tenants, felt the parish to be so sure of a good example, and the poor of the best attention and relief, that however sorry and ashamed for the necessity of the removal, she could not but in conscience feel that they were gone who deserved not to stay, and that Kellynch Hall had passed into better hands than its owners' (p. 141). With the traditional landed gentry going to seed and now festering in Bath, the defenders of England at sea now return to save the country from unwelcome internal social change by restoring and strengthening the old order. Anne's happy progress to a wedding with Wentworth represents the stirring victory of supremely reactionary forces, recognized, admired and greatly needed. Hence the novel's final sentences: 'His profession was all that could ever make her friends wish that tenderness less; the dread of a future war was all that could dim her sunshine. She gloried in being a sailor's wife, but she must pay the tax of quick alarm for belonging to that profession which is, if possible, more distinguished in its domestic virtues than in its national importance' (pp. 253–4). Important, too, because its 'domestic virtues' will now save the nation from change.

To clarify the various stages of the arguments and the conclusions they had developed in discussion, the students helped design another sheet, on the subject of 'Order and Repression v. Change', which was then typed up and distributed (by now the main points could be referred to by a somewhat

---

DIAGRAM 3   Order and Repression v. Change

I Role of women – 'no-thingness', etc. Accepted way of passing the time, and in need of a husband . . . Starts with 'girls and boys'	Could be used for a radical critique of the social order (causes illness, *ennui*, etc.)

But it isn't

<u>Repression</u>

2(a) Function of Navy in text	Reassertion of traditional values, 'domestic virtues', fit social leaders (*contra* decadence and snobbery of Bath and Sir W. Elliot). Naval marriages seem pleasant enough, but still in terms of patriarchy, old social roles
(b) Superior/Inferior 'social' discourse (cf. *Emma*)	Authorial discourse validates traditional social order This privileged discourse is shared by Anne: author and Anne represent and defend social and textual privilege
3 Anne's discourse repressed and not heeded by most other characters (including Lady Russell 7 years ago)	But 'doesn't matter because she gets her man in the end'. Her discourse is considered fine and is validated by Austen from the start (*contra* Emma's)

The text appears to reproduce the ideology at work in 2 and 3 in the interests of a textual and social 'order'.
What are the effects of the repressive ideology and social practices on the text itself? Can see the effects on women's lives in I, but this isn't really questioned by the ruling discourses.
Where else can we find the effects of this 'order'?

Look for oddities, 'disturbances', strange elements in the story of Anne's passage from

Prudence ⟶ Romance ⟶ Marriage

4 'Agitation' Time and again occurs as main feature of romance	Heightened, strained language and emotional reactions – serious case of 'disorder'. Extent of this agitation is a measure of the repression going on – and which the text doesn't want to admit to
5 Use of coincidence and luck: old order has to be saved by 'magic' – function of Mrs Smith	Mrs Smith needed in the text to salvage order – prevents undesirable 'disorder' of union between Anne and W. Elliot. Ensures Anne drops any interest in him and clears path for Wentworth

Use of magic and presence of severe outbreaks of 'agitation' suggest the established (and re-established) order isn't quite as neat and tidy as it appears

Emphasis upon the desirability of the old order = Anne doesn't need to change: she was right all along and at the close confirms her views of 7 years before: Anne too represents 'domestic virtue', so she is obviously ideally suited to the naval type (especially now he's rich and highly eligible)

(Note – Louisa is a bit too 'flighty' [disorder]: heading for a fall which will knock some sense into her and quieten her down)

elliptical code; see diagram 3). As well as using the incidences of sickness and agitation as a gauge of the extent to which an ordered textual and social system actually works in a repressive manner, the group also considered the function of Mrs Smith in the novel. Her purpose, through her use of past knowledge and her present intricate channels of communication, is to reveal to Anne, and the reader, the 'real' nature and interests of the attractive William Elliot, whose regard for Anne has awakened her flattered attention. By revealing his dastardly ways, Mrs Smith prevents Elliot sabotaging the desired, orderly closure: at the same time, however, as the group commented, the use of Mrs Smith, who fortuitously appears and acts as a insubstantial fairy-godmother-like figure, also reveals the extent to which the old order must rely on magic and luck if it is to be succesful in the struggle against deceit and change. The presence of Mrs Smith and the examples of disorder and sickness arising from repression reveal, therefore, some of the conflicts which the text cannot escape even as it works to produce a coherent representation of ideological health: the text, approached in this manner, was seen to 'express the contradictions of the social reality in which it was produced'.

After three weeks of intensive reading, discussion, note-making, designing sheets, and so on, the students completed their coursework folders by negotiating, planning and then writing an essay which would explain and extend some aspects of the work they had undertaken, using as a title 'For a novel so concerned with order, *Persuasion* seems strangely agitated . . . '.

In 1978, an A Level Examiner's Report was able to dismiss with a contemptuous sneer any attempt by students to deal with the politics of the texts they had studied:

> To get high marks, candidates must discuss such phrases as . . . 'intensity of poetic expression'. This precision was absent . . . when too much ink, if not thought, was wasted on unnecessary social history and even social protest . . . Ignorant abuse of the upper classes was no substitute for literary analysis and textual evidence.[32]

Although not often expressed with such confidence recently, a similar attitude still pervades much of A Level English. The two examples of classroom practice that we have discussed here have different emphases, resulting from the texts studied and their place in a two-year syllabus, but we hope that they indicate the possibility of a consistent, coherent method of teaching which, while still based firmly on 'literary analysis and textual evidence', also enables a full acknowledgement, exploration and understanding of the 'social history' without which 'literature' would have no meaning.

NOTES

1   We have discussed AEB 660 previously in our articles 'I See The Murderer Is A Skilful Door-Opener' in Peter Brooker and Peter Humm, eds. *Dialogue and Difference*, Routledge, 1989, and '"An Ordeal of Degrading Personal Compulsion": English 14-18' in *Changing the Subject: Literature Teaching Politics Journal – 6*, 1987, available from Peter Hawkins, Department of French, University of Bristol, 19 Woodland Road, Bristol BS8 1TE.
Avon branch of NATE is currently working on a Mode 3 A Level in Literary and Cultural Studies which, among other things, aims to avoid the problems inherent in AEB 660. For further details, see 'Challenging A Level' in *The English Magazine* 20, 1988 or write to AATE A Level Working Party c/o 16 Burlington Road, Redland, Bristol BS6 6TL.

2   Terry Eagleton, *Myths of Power: A Marxist Study of the Brontës*, Macmillan, 1975.

3   Ralph Fox, *The Novel and The People*, Lawrence & Wishart, 1937, reprinted 1979.

4   Boris Ford, 'An Analysis of *Wuthering Heights*', Scrutiny VII(4) 1939; Eagleton, *Myths of Power*; J. Hillis Miller, *Fiction and Repetition*, Blackwell, 1982.

5   A much simplified version of the reading in David Musselwhite, *Wuthering Heights: The Unacceptable Text*, Red Letters (2) 1976.

6   Ford, 'An Analysis of *Wuthering Heights*'.

7   James H. Kavanagh, *Rereading Literature: Emily Brontë*, Blackwell, 1985.

8   Q.D. Leavis, *Lectures in America*, Chatto, 1969.

 9 Sandra M. Gilbert and Susan Gubar, *The Madwoman in the Attic*, Yale University Press, 1979.
10 Keith Sagar, *Emily Brontë: Wuthering Heights*, British Council, 1975.
11 Stephen Jacobi, 'The Importance of Not Being Nelly', in Linda Cookson and Brian Loughry, eds., *Critical Essays on Wuthering Heights*, Longman, 1988.
12 Catherine Belsey, *Critical Practice*, Methuen, 1980.
13 Catherine Belsey, 'Literature, History, Politics', *Literature and History 9 (1), 1983.*
14 Pierre Macherey, 'Problems of Reflection', in Francis Barker et al., eds., *Literature, Society and the Sociology of Literature*, University of Essex, 1977.
15 Heather Glen, *Introduction to Wuthering Heights*, Routledge, 1988.
16 Hannah More, *Coelebs in Search of a Wife*, 1809.
17 William Grimshaw, 'The Admonition of a Sinner', quoted in Glen, *Introduction to Wuthering Heights*.
18 William Blake, *The Marriage of Heaven and Hell*, 1793.
19 *The Poor Man's Guardian*, 11 January 1934, quoted in Richard Johnson, 'Really Useful Knowledge' in John Clark et al., eds., *Working Class Culture*, Hutchinson, 1979.
20 Eva Figes, *Sex and Subterfuge*, Macmillan, 1982.
21 Ford, *'An Analysis of 'Wuthering Heights'*.
22 Leavis, *Lectures in America*.
23 Rosemary Jackson, *Fantasy: The Literature of Subversion*, Methuen, 1987.
24 Macherey, *'Problems of Reflection'*.
25 Emily Brontë, *Wuthering Heights*, Penguin, 1985, pp. 338–46.
26 Musselwhite, *Wuthering Heights*.
27 David Cecil, *A Portrait of Jane Austen*, Constable, 1978.
28 *An Interview With Pierre Macherey*, Red Letters 5, 1977.
29 Jane Austen, *Persuasion*, Penguin, 1985, p. 49. All subsequent page references are to this edition.
30 Terry Lovell, 'Jane Austen and Gentry Society' in Barker et al., eds., *Literature, Society and the Sociology of Literature*.
31 David Lodge, *Changing Places*, Penguin, 1978.
32 Examiner's Report on JMB A Level English, 1978.

9 The materialism of 'différance'
Paul Moran

1 I am presently an English teacher at Beauchamp Community College in Leicestershire. My interest in theory developed as a direct result of my experience of the institutional production of reading practices. The significance of theory within education surely resides within its exposure of the relationship between reading and institutional practices.

2 I never wanted to be an English teacher – I always wanted to be thin and muscular instead! I have always been embarrassed by this fact. This embarrassment is linked to the enormous influence which my father exerted over me as a father, a Communist and a trade union activist.

3 My father, an ex-Catholic and staunch Communist, sent me to a Church of England primary school, by which time I was theorized up to the hilt. I then went to a secondary modern school, a sixth form college and London University. It's all been very peculiar. I'm now an English teacher at Beauchamp Community College, and am also doing research at Leicester University.

I would like to explain 'différance' (see glossary) by way of a simplification, and in order to do this, I shall first of all have to quote a famous poem, and then afterwards quote what an academic critic has written about it.

> I wandered lonely as a cloud
> That floats on high o'er vales and hills,
> When all at once I saw a crowd,
> A host, of golden daffodils;
> Beside the lake, beneath the trees,
> Fluttering and dancing in the breeze.
>
> Continuous as the stars that shine
> And twinkle in the milky way,
> They stretched in never-ending line
> Along the margin of a bay;
> Ten thousand saw I at a glance,
> Tossing their heads in sprightly dance.

The waves beside them danced; but they
Out-did the sparkling waves in glee:
A poet could not but be gay,
In such a jocund company:
I gazed – and gazed – but little thought
What wealth the show to me had brought:

For oft, when on my couch I lie
In vacant or in pensive mood,
They flash upon that inward eye
Which is the bliss of solitude;
And then my heart with pleasure fills,
And dances with the daffodils.[1]

The flowers, though a part of the universal order, are still themselves, each an individual life asserting itself joyfully; 'tossing their heads' and 'sprightly dance' suggest the unconscious courage of the fragile lives so gaily lived out under the trees and under the stars. Yet each flower is part of a 'host' of 'ten thousand' which stretches in 'never-ending line'. The daffodils are not merely happily vegetating; they are joyously embattled in the wind. This is a point of crucial importance for the full appreciation of the poem . . . What Wordsworth invites us to remember with him, imprisoned in our solitudes, is the universal order of which we ourselves, the waves, the trees, the daffodils, and the stars are all individual parts. In imaginatively contemplating that order, we cease, for a moment of thought, to feel the burden of loneliness.[2]

One fine morning, during the spring term, in a place which is known as E2, I read Wordsworth's poem to one of my fourth-year groups. I bore in mind what Professor Durrant had written about the daffodils as parts of a universal order, and that by contemplating them in this way, through Wordsworth's poem, we could 'cease for a moment of thought, to feel the burden of loneliness'. I read the poem to the class for a second time and asked them to study their own copies individually for a few minutes. Dutifully, the class obeyed. 'Does anyone still feel lonely?' I asked. One or two of them did. 'Think about the daffodils', I suggested. 'Think what about them?' one of the lonely wanted to know.

'Just think about them', I said. 'It'll take your mind off things, he means', explained one of the others. As that wasn't quite what I meant, I explained the words of Professor Durrant to them by using a diagram I drew on the board.

'Anyway,' I said, after the explanation, 'it must have worked for most of you; only a few of you felt lonely after reading the poem.' Vasso was amongst many of those who complained that they weren't lonely to start with. 'Had you come across the poem before?' I asked. She'd heard of it, but had never read it the whole way through. 'Perhaps just hearing about it was enough', I suggested. Vasso wasn't convinced by this argument; she thought that, although Professor Durrant was 'probably clever' he was, nevertheless, 'talking crap'. It was at this point that I tended to disagree with Vasso about the first part of her statement.

If this had been all that was involved, I would have been quite happy to have let the matter rest with Vasso's eloquent words of dismissal. However, the problem – which is essentially the problem of 'différance' – and the circumstances through which the problem, became possible, were and are rather more complex. Why is it that Professor Durrant's expression of Wordsworth's poem, which has found itself reproduced in print, and is generally respected – if not necessarily agreed with – by an academic and literary establishment, can also be so appositely rejected as 'crap'? I am most certainly not prepared to dismiss what Vasso had to say. The grounds upon which her judgement of Professor Durrant's reading of the poem was based, appear, temptingly, to be demonstrably true. Wordsworth's poem had no significant effect upon the emotional state of the individuals of the class. His reading of the poem also implied that loneliness was the natural and universal condition of humanity. Again, this seemed not to be the case. However, within Professor Durrant's expressed understanding of 'I wandered lonely as a cloud', is also the explicit claim of more than his own experience and understanding of the poem: this claim is made present in a number of ways.

Durrant's universalizing of humanity through his reading of Wordsworth's poem is achieved by his interpretation of the flowers, the trees, the waves and the stars as metaphors for the individual human subject being identified by its innate membership of a general species, through which difference, and thus isolation, is annulled. The individual, by being conscious of what it belongs to, that is, by being conscious of what it is, is therefore able to find sanctuary from 'the burden of loneliness' which is its own individuality: contemplation of the poem in this way, according to Durrant, asserts this point of universality and the elimination of 'différance' – 'joyfully'. But then, what of Vasso? Surely Vasso's expression of herself, in the light of her reading of the poem, is such an expression of difference which Durrant's reading denies; not only of linguistic difference, but also cultural, social, educational, institutional and ideological difference? Vasso was adamant that she was not lonely. She was equally adamant that her lack of loneliness did not stem from her knowledge of 'I wandered lonely as a cloud'. Her own expressions of her difference in respect to Professor Durrant were palpably true: Durrant was male, Vasso was female; Durrant was a member of a university, Vasso was not going to university; Durrant wrote books and was interested in poetry, Vasso couldn't imagine that she would ever write a book and was not especially interested in poetry; Durrant led one kind of life, Vasso led another. Did this mean that Durrant's reading of the poem was incorrect? It turned out that in this respect Vasso was a lot more generous – 'He's got his view and I've got mine' – than Durrant is prepared to be.

Whilst Vasso was prepared to accept a diversity of readings of the poem, a diversity which is continuous with the material conditions of difference through which a reading is produced, Durrant emphasizes that his understanding of the poem is, and consequently represents, more than a particular point of view: the expression of the individual as a member of a universal order through which material difference is annulled is 'a point of crucial importance for the full understanding of the poem'. In effect, Professor Durrant is claiming that unless his point is accepted, the reader cannot have a full understanding of the text; in this way, without negating the material conditions of difference which collectively define the reader's identity and acquiescing to the sovereignty of the perspective from which Durrant's reading of the poem was produced, the reader is denied access to the full meaning of the poem. In the name of the full meaning of the poem, Vasso was being asked to negate those material differences which defined her as Vasso, material differences which must also include her expression of 'I wandered lonely as a cloud'.

The conceptual ground of full meaning and full understanding is authoritarian by claiming itself as Reason's self-determination: consequently it creates the dichotomy of self and other. The other, which Vasso represented, is dialectically opposed to the same, which Durrant represented in his reading of Wordsworth's poem. Specifically, full meaning, the concept which establishes this dialectical opposition – and classically there have been many names for the operation of this concept, such as Logos, History, the Idea, the Concept, the Free-Market Economy – denies the relevance of difference, which can only be expressed in and through the world; which is to say that difference can only occur materially. The expression of the concept of full meaning is therefore a denial of material relevance. What Durrant claims for his reading of the poem is the irrelevance of his or any reading of it; the reader, who could hardly be anything other than a material being engaged in the material activity of reading and the expression of reading, is deemed insignificant because the full meaning of the poem is present by itself within the text; the full meaning of the poem is perceived as being self-determinedly complete. If this were not the case, then Vasso's and any other reading of the poem could not be criticized on the grounds that it was not expressive of the full meaning of the poem; nor could there be any inside or outside of the text, which the concept that Durrant articulates also implies, on the grounds that the full meaning of the poem must be contained within the text, in an absolute sense, and does not vary according to the material conditions of the reader. In effect, without the articulation of the concept of Reason's self-determination and the presence of meaning within the poem, the dichotomy of same and other, and their dialectical opposition, would not exist. Unfortunately, this concept has and is being constantly articulated, not just by Durrant, but more potently by the general articulation of the subject of English and the processes of marking, grading and assessing which support this particular subject through the institution of the school. However, there is no effective reason why this articulation of meaning should not be expressed as such, as articulation, being materially constructed, rather than being present of and for itself – there is no reason why this deconstruction should not take place in schools and henceforth constitute what 'English' as a subject used to be. Vasso was quite keen on the idea. And while it is unlikely that such a deconstruction will immediately render the authority of English impotent, even though the ramifications of such a deconstruction in the field of the subject and its pedagogy are potentially far-reaching, the institutional structures which support it have been and probably will continue to be, embarrassed by what has been revealed. It is towards this ground, which is the denied materiality of the concept, that the subject of English must now shift.

As we have seen, Durrant articulates through his reading of the poem the concept of full meaning being present within the text by itself: the concept is expressed as being univalence, authenticity and innateness. In this way, through his expression of the poem, Durrant has effected a schism between himself and his expression. He has over-written his own reading of the poem with a writing that proclaims his own absence from what he has produced, from what he has read. By this means Durrant is able to grant a determined autonomy to the concept, to express its detachment from himself as itself: if we were to be concerned with Marxist thematics we should say that Durrant had fetishized the object of his labour in the form of the concept, and had become alienated from the production of meaning through the conception of textual presence. This would be to represent the limit of the text, the boundary which an interior (textual) meaning and the materiality of the world, which he peculiarly alludes to by way of the anonymity of the reader. But what are the possibilities of such a schism? Not of the schism being expressed – Durrant and others have done this most imperiously – but of the schism itself, the between of the articulation of the concept and the concept (itself)?

In one sense, which is, for the moment, the least recognized and acted upon aspect of the material sense, the possibility of the schism which Durrant expresses is entirely illusory. Durrant expresses not only the breaking away of the concept from the producer of the concept, but also the idea that the concept was effective before its expression, prior to its being identified: yet paradoxically, even if this were the case, which it is not, where and how would the concept be without its being expressed? In what way could it be identified without its being articulated through the material process of reading? In order for the concept to be, it must be articulated: this is the being of meaning, it resides, is present, entirely and only, through and within, its expression. In this sense, therefore, the schism which Durrant effects between himself and the concept of 'full understanding', and all which this must imply, is an affectation of himself; the material possibility of this schism is, in effect, an impossibility; what he establishes between himself and the concept is not a rift which is traversed by a dialogue with, and understanding of, the text of Wordsworth's poem, but a monologue of the concept and himself.

The subject of English often professes, as of course it should, a general concern with the dialogical and an examination of its processes; it particularly emphasizes the importance of the dialogical processes which occur between the student and the teacher, and the text and the reader. Clearly, however, the authoritarian concept of full meaning, which implies the valorization of a 'full understanding' against which other readings must be expressed as incomplete and therefore inferior, is hardly able to engage in any real dialogic process. Instead, as we have unfortunately just witnessed, Professor Durrant is much more concerned with establishing the apparatus that would allow him to have intercourse with himself, a seemingly impossible task which is made more problematic by Professor Durrant's desire to impose this 'monology' upon others in an attempt to make them the same. This authoritarian desire is essentially concerned with establishing the repetition of itself, which can only be achieved by imposing and maintaining control of its own discourse.

In English, the procedures which enact this desire are institutionalized, and include marking, grading and examining. In this way, the polysynonymy of difference is avoided: meetings take place, criteria are discussed and, one way or another, students and their work are determined as being anything from a G to an A. The material differences through which work is produced are ignored; indeed, the material differences which the grades themselves bespeak are perceived as being the natural, univalent and innate meaning of the work which has been produced. In this sense, the impossible schism between the articulation of the concept (itself), between the expression of meaning and the presence of meaning (within the poem, and within the subject of English) has been effected; for it is only on these grounds, of the 'full understanding' of a text, (which uncompromisingly speaks of its independent full meaning, that is present already, prior to its location through the activity of reading) that any grade other than A can be awarded. Any other mark indicates a failure to achieve this 'full understanding', it is a mark which is more than analogous to the mark of the fall from the presence of grace. A good job might depend on such a mark, and its indication of the extent to which one has fallen.

The special way in which the schism has been presented, as that which maintains the autotelos, or self-presence, of full meaning, which resides independently within the interiority of the text and is more generally the autotelos which legitimates and constitutes the subject and its other, and so also designates the exteriority of the material world and determines all dialectical oppositions, that singular and all-important ordering schism, can only ever be presented, that is, can only ever be expressed and maintained materially, through the exposition of material difference. We decided to examine more closely what this involved, and in order to do this we had to take another, closer look at the poem. (Although there might perhaps be some thematic neatness in using Wordsworth's poem to demonstrate ideas which are connected with presence, being and meaning, any example of writing could be used to this end.)

We started by examining and discussing a number of questions in relation to the poem:

1   Are there a lot of daffodils?
2   Where are the daffodils?

3   Do any of the trees look dead?
4   Who is looking at the daffodils?
5   Are they wearing brown shoes?
6   Is the ground too wet for a picnic?
7   Does it look like it is going to rain?
8   What is the person on the couch doing with their hands?
9   Does the person on the couch prefer drinking strong lager to fancy tea?
10   Daffodils usually have yellow petals and green stems, but so do many other flowers such as sunflowers and dandelions: how do you know that the flowers which are being looked at are not really sunflowers?

Taken as a whole, the questions did not prove to be unproblematic. 'I don't know what he's doing with his hands', was a common and insistent reply. 'But if you know where the daffodils are, why can't you tell me where his hands are and what he's doing with them?' A certain exasperation followed, after which came the exclamation, 'Because they aren't really there!'

'Where are they?' I persisted. 'If they aren't there, where can they be? Are you saying that the person has no hands?' No, they weren't saying that he had no hands. But if this was the case, why couldn't they locate them?

Other questions caused not dissimilar problems. 'How can you be certain', I asked, 'that the poem is really about daffodils? How do you know that the person is really looking at daffodils and not dandelions?' A large number of the class concluded, like Vasso, that the meaning of the poem depended upon how the individual interpreted its meaning. But how was such a situation possible? Why did meaning appear to be indeterminate? 'If', I asked, 'you could actually talk to the person on the couch, if you could actually go there, would that solve our problems about meaning?' Some of the class thought that our problems could indeed be solved in this way. 'So why can't we go there, then?' I wondered. There were a number of answers to this question, three of which appear to be especially significant:

1   You might have been able to go there once, but that was in the past and was to do with when the poem was written, and was about where the poem was written
2   You could not go there because the place does not exist
3   You could not go there because the place was in the poem and the poem was only words

All three of the above answers are connected with Derridean notions of 'différance', which contains in a special way the verbs to differ and to defer, and effectively deconstructs the autotelos or self-presence of meaning and being. As a class we went on to discuss and write about some of the implications of these answers. We were particularly concerned with how, through language, being and meaning become dislocated, and also with the meaning of language as a reference to being, which it clearly was itself unable to be.

We devised and discussed numerous ways in which this could be demonstrated. Words and sentences were written on the board and on bits of paper: someone wrote the word 'gun' on the board, and the point was made that the word 'gun' was not the gun itself, that language was a reference to being. We produced short pieces of writing about written statements which, because of the absence of a single and fixed referent, made meaning problematic; statements such as 'I am here' and 'I love you', even when originally produced with a referent in mind, are still subject to the problem of meaning being produced – of the text being read – in accordance with different material conditions. Indeed, the importance of different material conditions became especially emphasized when it was pointed out that the students' own writing would inevitably be subjected to a form of scrutiny which denied not only the theoretical importance of what they were writing about, despite their close scrutiny of the texts with which they had been concerned, but also denied the very different material conditions themselves which produced such different (readings of) texts. This denial of 'différance' would operate through the grading of coursework folders, and was itself maintained through a variety of material structures, which included the institution of the subject. What, they wanted to know, are we going to do about this state of affairs? Well, what are we?

NOTES

1   William Wordsworth, 'I wandered lonely as a cloud'.

2   G. Durrant, *Wordsworth and the Great System: A Study of Wordsworth's Poetic Universe*, Cambridge University Press, 1970, pp. 131–3.

10 The curious English teacher's guide to modern literary theories

To say literary theory started at any particular time or date would be naive, yet as with any movement or set of ideas it is possible to unearth the traces by reference to its socio-historical provenance. The great surge of scientific rationalism which characterized the later nineteenth century faded with the onset of the twentieth, prompted by the diffusion of new technologies throughout industrial societies. Music and art strained to accommodate new forms, and literature became locked in an intense probing of its raw material, language. Joseph Conrad's *Heart of Darkness*, published in 1902, takes this issue, the limits of understanding that a rational industrialized culture can encompass when faced with the appalling consequences of its own barbarism, and in the end, 'the issue is transposed on to a metaphysical level.'[1] Conrad does not have the language available to interrogate the white colonialists' experience of African people in material, historical terms, as David Murray's incisive article makes clear.

Also in 1902, just before the Wright brothers lurched off the surface of the earth, a key document of the crisis in language that European culture suffered was published. This was the Lord Chandos Letter, written by the German writer Hofmannsthal as a cry from the heart of his own personal and creative darkness. His medium has failed him; all the certainties of a society encoded in unambiguous and living language structures have been eroded in a crisis of confidence in the possibility of language saying anything significant at all. As a writer he can clutch at ciphers like a rusting harrow in a field, or a mangy dog; these 'broken images' signify, while the encoded tradition is empty, moribund. There were other witnesses to the language 'crisis', such as Ludwig Wittgenstein, who probed to its atomic limits, as he first thought, 'the totality of propositions' which 'is language'.[2] The preoccupation with form is a consequence of the loss of trust in language's ability to construct a stable view of a radically changing world. It is manifested throughout early modernist writing – 'Prufrock', 'The Waste Land', *Women in Love, Mrs Dalloway, Ulysses,* all explore their own discourse structures from differing standpoints. In the early years of the twentieth century, then, language was held up to the light and found opaque. It was not a window on experience, but it appeared to constrain it. Therefore its formal properties presented themselves as variables for writers to experiment with.

Russian formalists lay literature bare!

This general attitude towards form found expression in pre-revolutionary Russia in the work of the writers known today as the Russian formalists. Some of the most well-known names from the writers in Russia are Roman Jakobson, Viktor Shklovsky, Boris Eichenbaum and Yuri Tynyanov. Jakobson had a very long career, moving to Prague in the late nineteen-twenties and finally to the USA. This group is not in fashion among academics, but for the teacher of English their theories offer some interesting ways into texts without the difficult intellectual games that some later theorists appear to entail. Their most important concept is probably 'defamiliarization'; this involves the ways in which literary texts use language differently from ordinary, everyday speech. The result for the reader is to have his or her perception slowed down. In T.S. Eliot's 'The Waste Land' the effect of defamiliarization is felt from the first line; 'April is the cruellest month'. Our vernal associations of sweet showers and lambs gambolling take a tumble on reading this. Indeed the whole poem is riddled with defamiliarizing moments:

> That corpse you planted last year in your garden
> Has it begun to sprout?
> Will it bloom this year?

For some texts, then, the concept of defamiliarization is an immediate entry point, a way of tackling the difficulties. It is obviously applicable to poetic texts, and particularly those from the twentieth century, although the metaphors of Shakespeare could be profitably examined from this frame of reference. Obviously prose texts also defamiliarize. Take the opening of Salman Rushdie's *Midnight's Children*: 'I was born in the city of Bombay . . . once upon a time. No, that won't do, there's no getting away from the date.' And, from a more conventional text, Thomas Hardy's *The Return of the Native*:

> The spot was, indeed, a near relation of night, and when night showed itself an apparent tendency to gravitate together could be perceived in its shades and the scene. The sombre stretch of rounds and hollows seemed to rise and meet the evening gloom in pure sympathy, the heath exhaling darkness as rapidly as the heavens precipitated it. And so the obscurity in the air and the obscurity in the land closed together in a black fraternization towards which each advanced half-way.[3]

The problem with defamiliarization is that it appears to be unable to account for literary devices losing their defamiliarizing capacity. When does the scandalously avant-garde become part of everyday perceptions? Take, for example, the film techniques used in *Elvira Madigan* to portray the lovers against the natural background; they now appear in shampoo and chocolate commercials, part of our habitual viewing. To solve this difficulty, the formalists developed the distinction between device and function. It is how the device works in the text that becomes of interest. Why for instance does the text of Dickens' *Our Mutual Friend* use the present tense for the chapters dealing with the Veneerings? The formalists further added to their ideas by using the notion of foregrounding, and of the dominant. Whatever device is foregrounded by the text, that is, brought to the notice of the reader, will become the dominant.

This can be quite complex in its patterning, as Halliday's analysis of William Golding's *The Inheritors* shows. Halliday analyses the syntactic structures of the novel, showing how certain options in clause structure are foregrounded, those to do with the way the speaker 'encodes his experiences of the external world, and of the internal world of his own consciousness, together with the participants in these processes and their attendant circumstances.'[4] Thus in a key passage the Neanderthal Lok is hiding in bushes watching the more advanced proto-humans called the tribe. One of the tribe sees him, draws a bow and shoots an arrow at him. Lok sees the situation in a series of unconnected fragments:

> Suddenly Lok understood that the man was holding the stick [bow] out to him but neither he nor Lok could reach across the river . . . The stick began to grow shorter at both ends. Then it shot out to full length again . . . His ears twitched and he turned to the tree. By his face there had grown a twig: a twig that smelt of other, and of goose, and of the bitter berries that Lok's stomach told him he must not eat.[5]

To shorten Halliday's detailed and careful analysis, the Neanderthal does not have a conception of a world of cause and effect. This is shown by the dominant syntactic options selected in the text. Lok's tragedy is that the only time he does act upon the world is when he snatches one of the tribe in a last desperate gesture. In Halliday's words, 'The action gets him nowhere; but it is a syntactic hint that his people have played their part in the long trek towards the human condition.'[6] Russian formalism offers, through its concepts of defamiliarization, foregrounding of the device, and the dominant, some straightforward entry points into the linguistic patterns of a text for the reader.

Structuralism rises from Saussure's sign

While concentrating on language and linguistic insights which have underpinned literary theories, I have to bring in the work of Ferdinand de Saussure. He was a Swiss linguist working in Geneva in the years preceding the 1914–18 war. From his lectures, a group of his students put together a book published in 1916 as *Course in General Linguistics*. It is from this book that many of the more startling developments in literary theories derive. Of course it must be said that the general climate of discourse was very favourable to the position held by Saussure; if it had not been his theory, someone else would have produced a similar position. The main proposal of Saussure's linguistics is that language is a system made up of signs which are arbitrary and differential.

First, the sign: one element, a sound image, or its written version, is united with a concept, which forms the other element; the two together form the sign. Saussure called the first the signifier and the second the signified. Put like that it's very abstract; in concrete terms, when we hear the sound image 'dog' we have a corresponding concept of dog. Now it is not some essential or supercanine that is being evoked in this sign; it is just that in our language the signifier 'dog' is used by English speakers as an agreed categorization of domestic canines, as opposed to 'wolf', for example. There is an important implication in this position; there is no natural link between the signifier 'dog' and the concept dog. It is arbitrary and conventional. It might have been the case that in English the signifier for the concept dog was 'zog'. There would still be dogs in our lives, but we would think and speak them through a different sign. This point is not too hard to take in, but there is another implication of Saussure's linguistics which is tougher: the relationship of the sign to the 'real world' as also arbitrary and conventional.

If we stay with our canine, an important determining factor on its meaning is its place in the linguistic system; 'dog' is not 'cat' or 'bat' or 'rat'. So its meaning isn't an act of positive identification but a placing from a range of entry conditions in a system of differences. The system is the language system – in Saussure's term, *langue* – which is structurally organized along two axes, the syntagmatic, and the paradigmatic. The first term refers to the language chain, which most teachers are aware of as sentence structure, although it also includes the rules for combining phonemes. The second term refers to the sets of items that can be chosen to fit in the links of the chain; consider 'April is the cruellest month' – clearly 'cruellest' could be replaced by such adjectives as 'sweetest', 'sunniest', 'silliest', and so on, with a little metrical licence. The point is that the structural slot, along the syntagmatic axis, is dying for an adjective to fill it. In literary texts the associative function of the paradigmatic axis is particularly exploited by poetry. Try some alternatives for 'I _____ lonely as a _____' or 'O to _____ loose,' or 'lucent _____, tinct with _____, or anything else you fancy. There is a clear route into poetic diction from this seemingly innocent patterning, for all ages.

Any individual utterance selects from the system of *langue* and gains meaning by its difference from other utterances, and from all other possible utterances. *Parole*, as Saussure termed it, is interesting to the linguist only in its relationships with *langue*. Similarly, for literary texts, what is interesting to the Saussurian, or structural analyst, is the relationship of individual and total patterns. In practice, the situation is not quite as formalistic as it appears from the brief summary. Roland Barthes' early work *Mythologies* analyses all manner of things in a structuralist framework. The focus on a margarine advert gives rise to this:

> One can trace in advertising a narrative pattern which clearly shows the working of this new vaccine (the inoculation of the public with a contingent evil to prevent or cure an essential one). It is found in the publicity for Astra margarine. The episode always begins with a cry of

indignation against margarine: 'A mousse? Made with margarine? Unthinkable! Your uncle will be furious!' And then one's eyes are opened, one's conscience becomes more pliable, and margarine is a delicious food, tasty, digestible, economical, useful in all circumstances. The moral at the end is well known: 'Here you are, rid of a prejudice which cost you dearly!'[7]

Barthes goes on to show how the Established Order in general uses this technique of inoculation – the army, church, government has little faults which can be admitted so as to make the public accept the general good of the institution concerned.

The study of narrative patterns in texts has been the most fruitful outcome of structuralist thought for most English teachers. One of the most effective examples is to be found in two English Centre publications, *Making Stories* and *Changing Stories*. While the level of difficulty of these texts locates them in the top junior classroom or the first year of an 11–16/18 secondary school, the conceptual frameworks, drawn from structuralist insights, can be adapted with a sophistication factor progressively added for older readers. The area of study, of narrative structures, is usually called narratology, and a useful short introduction to some of the issues has been written by Harold Rosen, in *Stories and Meanings;* he mentions particularly the work of Gerard Genette.

Another writer who is useful to the English teacher is Umberto Eco, who writes from a more sophisticated, but richer viewpoint than is shown in some earlier structuralist works such as Todorov's *Introduction to Poetics*. In *The Role of the Reader* he analyses the James Bond novels of Ian Fleming in terms of their narrative structure. According to Eco, the texts work at five levels:

1. the opposition of characters and values;
2. play situations and the story as a 'game';
3. a Manichean ideology; [good and evil as equally opposed forces]
4. literary techniques;
5. literature as collage.[8]

Eco shows how the Bond novels are built from a series of oppositions such as 'Bond–M', 'Bond–Villain', 'Villain–Woman', 'Woman–Bond', 'Free World–Soviet Union', 'Great Britain–Non-Anglo-Saxon countries'. In the analysis, the 'Bond–Villain' opposition is described thus: 'Bond represents Beauty and Virility as opposed to the Villain, who often appears monstrous and sexually impotent.' Eco then lists the villains in terms of physical characteristics such as Dr No, without hands, but with pincers; Goldfinger, who has been put together, as it were, 'with bits of other peoples' bodies', and so on. Further, the Villain is shown as ethnically marked, usually from central Europe or the Slav countries or the Mediterranean area, and of mixed blood. The woman fares pretty badly also. 'The general scheme is 1) the girl is beautiful and good; 2) she has been made frigid and unhappy by severe trials suffered in adolescence; 3) this has conditioned her to the service of the Villain; 4) through meeting Bond she appreciates her positive human chances; 5) Bond possesses her but in the end loses her'.[9] The Bond novel storylines function just like games with moves for each stage. Eco analyses *Diamonds Are Forever* in these terms (pp. 157–9 of *The Role of the Reader*). His acute summary shows that 'The novels of Fleming exploit in exemplary measure that element of foregone play which is typical of the escape machine geared for the entertainment of the masses . . . such machines represent the narrative structure which works upon a material which does not aspire to express any ideology.'[10] So to ideology; Fleming 'seeks elementary oppositions; to personify primitive and universal forces, he has recourse to popular standards . . . his is the static, inherent, dogmatic conservatism of fairy tales and myths, which transmit an elementary wisdom, constructed and communicated by a simple play of light and shade, by indisputable archetypes which do not permit critical distinction'.[11] Thus the names of his protagonists suggest mythical qualities. 'One obsessed by gold is called Auric Goldfinger. A wicked man is called No. . . . Ingenuity [i.e. an ingénue–Ed.] is suggested by the name of Honeychile; sensual shamelessness, by that of Pussy Galore'.[12]

Eco's final categories are discussed with clarity and sharp pointing. He demonstrates how Fleming's digressions serve to seduce the reader's literary pretensions by dwelling on the everyday and familiar; 'fifteen pages dedicated to a game of golf . . .' [13] This is, according to Eco, 'because it is with the familiar that he [Fleming] can solicit our capacity for identification.'[14] For the last category Eco traces Fleming's literary sources. This last enterprise is perhaps less easily applicable to the average classroom situation, but could well yield dividends for examination work.

The frameworks Eco adopts for his analysis stem from the basic structuralist principle of binary opposition, of *langue* to *parole*, of good and bad, hero(ine) and villain(ess), active and passive, dark and light, and so on. There is no reason why the technique cannot be applied to works of acknowledged literary merit – D.H. Lawrence argued in his *Study of Thomas Hardy* for the strength of the male–female duality and the principle may be seen at work in *Women in Love* particularly; for an example using William Blake's 'The Tyger', see Paul Bench's article. Similarly the notion of basic narrative structures can be employed from the infant class on.

Watch out! Post-structuralists are advancing on all flanks!

Now, just as you were settling down to your third cup of coffee to digest that lot, I am afraid I shall have to unsettle you again by moving on to what is in many ways an obvious development from structuralist approaches to literature, post-structuralist thought. If we recap on the Saussurian notion of language, we'll remember the sign was not in any obvious way related to the 'real world'. That meant that literary texts were patterns of signs in structures, or codes, which the reader assimilated into his or her own codes–'recuperated' is Culler's term.[15] Thus they were not windows onto the world, or the writer's mind, or good for your morals. They could be unpacked without deep feelings being violated, or a refusal to acknowledge a different position; patterns were available for all to see. In this 'objective' aspect, structuralist approaches offer English teachers ways into texts that do not depend on the inculcation of any particular sensibility or delicate powers of discrimination.

However, the very stability of the sign which makes structuralist thought possible was latched onto by the post-structuralists as a weak link in the Saussurian picture. For in Saussure's description of the sign there is a split: between signifier and signified. He argued for the indissoluble relationship of the two, once established in a language. Yet the two strata of the sign can be shown to be in an unstable relation, like layers of rock at fault-lines in the earth's crust. Looking at a dictionary reveals an important gap between signifier and signified. Raman Selden's example is useful: 'not only do we find for every signifier several signifieds (a "crib" signifies a manger, a child's bed, a hut, a job, a mine-shaft lining, a plagiarism, a literal translation, discarded cards at cribbage), but each of the signifieds becomes yet another signifier which can be traced in the dictionary with its own array of signifieds ("bed" signifies a place for sleeping, a garden plot, a layer of oysters, channel of a river, a stratum).'[16]

One immediate consequence of the prising apart of the two parts of the sign is that meaning becomes less fixed as a code, but much more a play of signifiers which won't be held down. Texts become plural and open; the universe of language is exponentially expanding, and truth, among other things, is problematized. How can you tell if you've arrived at the truth if your tools of analysis are themselves slippery, if the words of your enquiry slide away from verification at the last moment? Roland Barthes puts it this way: 'Any text is a new tissue of past citations. Bits of codes, formulae, rhythmic models, fragments of social languages, etc., pass into the text and are redistributed within it, for there is always language before and around the text.'[17] Apart from being an accurate description of Eliot's poetic technique, this passage should cue us into an aspect of structuralist thought that many critics have noted: it is dehistoricized; isolating a system involves taking it out of time altogether, so that it can be analysed under a still microscope, or regarding it as an arbitrary segment of an ongoing process of change. In this it resembles New Criticism, (see 'English Studies revisited'), the text lying meekly before the pure anatomical knife of the analyst's objectivity. The importance of the 'intertextuality' of the text which Barthes refers to must be emphasized; it casts a new light on originality, in its Romantic version of the inspired individual artist, as something of a fetish. It also brings in the reader as producer of meaning, who works to (re)write the text anew. In Barthes' view the reader is given infinite freedom to read the text in whatever way seems appropriate. Since language is always before and around the text, this will include the discourses of history and of the material circumstances of the reader. It is from this point that strategies for making readers in classrooms able to confront and interrogate texts can emerge.

There are some implications for the status of the 'author' in the reader's new freedom. The term is no longer necessarily 'white middle-class male authority' hovering at the back of the words we read. I recognize that in some classrooms, especially those using recent fiction written for children, this notion of the author may not be current. Yet it still dominates English Literature courses at A Level and upwards, particularly in the older establishments of Higher Education. If, then, the author, and what 'he' means, are taken away from the foreground of English teaching, the strategies open to the reader are much more varied. The text itself is not a sacred object, but an arena of play and invention. The number of possible texts that can be used also increases; since the idea of Great Literature has been exposed by the post-structuralists as a myth of a power élite, then there is a chance for popular texts, from, say, Catherine Cookson to television 'soaps' such as *Eastenders*; there is no reason why media texts should not be studied. Dennis Potter's television film *The Singing Detective* presents a challenge to an A Level group at once far more complex than Henry James and yet more accessible, since reading television is a natural part of the cultural practices of our pupils. We could say it creates the intertextual set towards texts which Classics provided pre-Arnoldian man (not, at any price, woman – Anne Elliot gives the definitive view: 'If you please, no reference to examples in books. Men have had every advantage of us in telling their own story. Education has been theirs in so much a higher degree; the pen has been in their hands.'[18]

Apart from freeing the teacher from the shadow of Leavis, adopting post-structuralist ways of using texts is an enabling strategy for the pupils. The articles by Cathy Twist and Paul Bench show how younger secondary children are brought to an active engagement with texts through the teacher's use of ideas from theorists such as Roland Barthes to guide their work. The theory does not prescribe; it opens out possible actions. It is in this sense that modern literary theories are liberating and enabling. Of course the teacher has to read some theories first and decide what ideas might be useful in planning 3p1's term's work on, say, Susan Hill's *Strange Meeting* or World War I poetry – including that by women, such as found in *Scars Upon My Heart* (Virago). She or he also has to operate from a stance of co-operative exploration with the children; the role of authority is not inscribed in her interpretative power, as if she were a priestess, but in her facilitation of the pupils' power as readers/writers.

Roland Barthes figures largely in the scene of post-structuralist reference because of the profusion and critical applicability of his writing. Paul Bench describes the use of his codes which a reader can employ to enter a text productively. The source for these codes is *S/Z*, a work which Barthes published in 1970. In this Barthes proclaimed a new, active reading which would not assign a single meaning to a text, but 'appreciate the plural of which it is fashioned'.[19] He takes a novella by Balzac, *Sarrasine*, divides it into reading units (lexias) and each unit is read through the grid of five codes (see pages 48-9). As well as the work Paul Bench describes, I'd like to draw your attention to a very interesting use of the Barthes codes in *Literary Theory at*

Work (see note 1). Elaine Millard analyses *St Mawr*, by D. H. Lawrence, from a feminist appropriation of the reading codes.[20] Her work points in further directions for texts studied at higher levels.

It would be impossible to offer any survey of post-structuralist work, however brief, without considering its most notorious concept, deconstruction. This term is usually associated with the French philosopher Jacques Derrida, who has in general upset the philosophical apple-cart with his scandalous pronouncements on issues such as truth and the possibility of guaranteeing you know when you have found it. These issues are beyond the scope of this book, but some of Derrida's ideas are of interest and can be applied in school, as Paul Moran's article shows. The notion of différance deconstructs our fondly held illusions of fully guaranteed unified meaning. It signals difference – remember Saussure's notion of meaning: cat is not bat is not hat is not rat – and it signals deferral. Look back at Selden's dictionary entry for 'crib'. Derrida's term is also interesting because its identity is only apparent in writing; in the spoken language it is indistinguishable from 'difference'.

One of Derrida's main complaints about Western thought, from Plato onwards, is its emphasis on the presence of the voice, the spoken language, as a guarantee of its authority, of an originary force which acts as a centre, or goal of our quest for understanding. Writing is seen as the junior partner in the pair Speech/Writing; it is secondary. Worse, it has a materiality of its own which detracts from the presence value of the writer. What Derrida does is to show that both speech and writing are processes of signification which both defeat a full understanding. Behind both is différance, the play of differentiation and deferral which has no beginning and no end. As we shall see, this idea was already worked in a somewhat different form by the Russian writer Bakhtin in the 1930s. We might contrast the absolute privileging of presence by Leavis in his formulation of 'This – doesn't it? – bears such a relation to that; this kind of thing – don't you find it so? – wears better than that.' Paul Moran's article shows up very graphically the critical terrorism of the Leavisite approach.

So to deconstruction. It is a twofold enterprise. On the basis that no text has full meaning or presence, read it closely and look for the gaps, the small holes at its seams; each text will offer points for the deconstructive reader to expose its contradictions, to show that the apparent coherence is an effect without any grounding. Take Yeats' 'Among School Children'. The last line, 'How can we know the dancer from the dance?' is usually understood to emphasize the potential unity between form and experience or, in the terms we have been using, the signifier and signified. Paul de Man, a deconstructive critic, shows how we can read the last line literally as opposed to figuratively, that is as an urgent cry for an answer, instead of a conventional rhetorical question which the text of the poem itself has already answered.[21] Or take the last page of *Women in Love*; the resolution of the Ursula/Birkin relationship is taken by many critics as affirmative; the stuggles of the novel's individual protagonists in the face of a disintegrating society, the tragedy of one who could not love and is dead, are forgotten in the quiet happiness of the close. This is to read this text as if it were *Little Dorrit*. Birkin's words 'I don't believe that', read as a moment of deconstruction, prise apart the binary opposition upon which the scaffolding of the novel appears to have been built. The text's moments of closure are shown to be only points in a continuing struggle. Male/female can, by the text's own admission, be read as the Derridean violent hierarchy it always has been – a sitte of struggle glossed over as natural by the accepted order of the words in which the first term of a pair is always 'superior'.

Deconstruction recognizes the problem of trying to use language as if it were transparent, as if the meanings which a text produced were full and guaranteed. It enables a reader to face even the most awesomely complex or authoritative texts without submitting to their authority. There is no denying the difficulty of some of the work of Derrida, de Man, Harold Bloom, in particular. However, as Paul Moran's article shows, it is possible to take a strategy of discourse such as différance and create work on texts which a conventional reading, demanding The Meaning, would not admit.

The work of Jacques Lacan is often mentioned in the same context as that of Derrida. He was a psychoanalyst who took a particular interest in language and its relation to the unconscious, and thus also to the construction of subjectivity, or identity. His own writing is very difficult, but his main ideas have been made available from a number of sources, including books on literary theories. He concentrates on the speaking subject. Let us consider first what we do when we speak of ourselves and others. Take the following utterance: 'I'll walk on. Where shall I meet you?' and the reply, 'I'll see you at the pub.' The first 'I' becomes 'you' in the reply, but the ego which asked the question remains the same. So language always offers the individual a series of subject positions – sometimes 'I', sometimes 'you', sometimes as object, 'Girl number twenty!' We accept this split between the subject of the narrated event, or enounced, and the subject of the linguistic act, or enunciation, as part of the communication process. Putting this another way, the subject of the enounced is always a grammatical function, whereas the subject of the enunciation is the person producing the meaning from the stretch of language, whatever form it is in.

The split which language institutes in our subjectivity as a condition of entry is taken up by Lacan in terms of the development of the ego. Before language enters a child's life, the child has an illusion of wholeness as if it were looking into a mirror. As at this stage the child is still governed by the pleasure principle, desire is not repressed but gives back a confirmation of satisfaction at being whole; but the mirror image is precisely that of an image which is only an illusion, and it is actually separate from the child. When the reality principle steps in and prevents the realization of the child's Oedipal desires, desire is repressed into the unconscious and the child develops language, in which she or he is split along various subject positions. So desire is never satisfied; it runs along the chain of signifiers, which are themselves unstable, not welded to their signifieds, which slide away denying stability. So 'I' stands at this intersection point where the two axes of signifier and signified should meet, but somehow always miss each other. How on earth, we might ask, is any communication in language possible?

Lacan's answer to this is the Phallus. Rather obscurely, it is not a physical object but a privileged signifier which dictates the law. It is in submission to this law that we speak; although we have transferred from the imaginary (mirror) stage to symbolic (language) stage, it is the language of others that shapes our understanding of ourselves. We are thus strung out along a signifying chain which endlessly displaces meanings, never allowing a full, final centredness. Luis Buñuel's films *The Phantom of Liberty* and *That Obscure Object of Desire* explore this dilemma in a most entertaining way.

Two further ideas from Lacan need to be inserted here: the roles of metaphor and metonymy. Metaphor is the favourite figure of lyric poetry in particular; it is a matter of correspondences, one signifier being transposed to another. As Lacan writes, 'The creative spark of the metaphor. . . .flashes between two signifiers, one of which has taken the place of the other in the signifying chain. . .'.[22] (See Barbara Johnson in the bibliography.) By way of contrast, metonymy is the figure which in classical definitions refers to the whole by mentioning an aspect of a whole and implying that whole by contextual association. So if you think of a fleet of ships, 'thirty sails' can easily be understood to refer, by metonymy, to the whole fleet. The interesting aspect of metonymy is the way Roman Jakobson, the Russian formalist who emigrated to the USA by way of Prague, extended the original idea to the syntagmatic axis of language.[23] If you can remember, the syntagmatic axis of language is the stringing out bit, the formal arrangement by which we are able to relate our topic to the act or thought or feeling it participates in – the cat (sat on the mat) (ate its dinner) (was run over by the man on the Clapham omnibus) (wore an inscrutable smile) – *ad infinitum*. Now if you can have all these structural substitutes for just one sentence type you can make infinite variations in your verbal planning; equally you can never settle: you are always searching, however much you hope you have the right order at last. And so Lacan takes up Jakobson's ideas to remind us how language in its chaining aspect, which yet could always be other, expresses desire. Metaphor is the perfect state of being, wholeness laid upon wholeness (see glossary). Metonymy is the strung out search of language in search of wholeness, and as such induces an inquiring mood in the reader/speaker. The use of these ideas for teaching English is quite extensive once the initial resistance to their strangeness is overcome. For they are acknowledging a fact of our own existence which we would often like to forget, namely that we exist in the world of language through a variety of positions (see Paul Bench's article, para. 1).

The position offered by a particular text addresses the reader as a subject so that a sense of identity is created by the text's play with the figures of metaphor and metonymy. T.S. Eliot's 'Four Quartets' is organized around such tensioning frames; it seems to move through a variety of positions for the reader to produce meaning from, only to culminate in 'the fire and the rose are one', a closing metaphor. The reader has been taken through a wide range of positions, of ways of seeing the world, which hover between the metaphorical or the metonymic. The metaphorical gives a sense of finality, of assimilating one thing with another. The metonymic does not offer a final position and keeps the open feel of the poem going. Yet all the exploration is terminated with the closure, the cut-off point, of the ending in a unified figure: the fire and the rose together.

Salman Rushdie exploits the notion of metonymy most amusingly at the beginning of *Midnight's Children,* with the courtship of Naseem by Aadam Aziz. As a doctor he has to examine his patient, but in strict religious fashion she cannot be revealed in her entirety. So he examines her through a hole in a sheet. She develops many so-called ailments, and thus he begins to have a picture of her as

> a badly fitting collage of her severally-inspected parts: . . . and pajamas fall from the celestial rump, which swells wondrously through the hole. Aadam Aziz forces himself into a medical frame of mind . . . reaches out . . . feels. And swears to himself, in amazement, that he sees the bottom reddening in a shy, but compliant blush.[24]

Metaphor is a figural attempt to effect closure, as in Yeats' poem 'Byzantium':

> Marbles of the dancing floor
> Break bitter furies of complexity
> Those images that yet
> Fresh images beget,
> That dolphin-torn, that gong-tormented sea

– the syntax piles image on image, creating a sense of finality in the repeated, overlaid metaphor. Metonymy involves a linear narrative of the self, which can be liberating. Billy Caspar, in Barry Hines' *A Kestrel for a Knave,* has no narratives of his self which are listened to by others, until his moment of acceptance in the English lesson, his narrative about hawks. He has a place, a safe house for his fragile identity to rest. But, true to the Lacanian world view, the house is built of cards.

One further area to explore from the Lacanian theory of language and the self is the way in which women are constructed by being made to produce meaning from texts. I shall say more about this in the section on feminist theories, but for the moment suggest that the romantic novel might be a fruitful focus for study.

A Marxist manifold

Marxist theories of literature have been influential for some sixty years. Marx himself said little about literature directly, but his views on the economic and social formations of societies underscore all Marxist theories of literature. In many ways these theories are easier to grasp and to apply in teaching texts than those from the post-structuralist field. Georg Lukács was the first well-known Marxist to influence Western writers, with his studies of the historical novel. He argued that texts which reflected the totality of a society in its historical struggles were the best. Notice he has a clear notion of value written into his system. He also has a view of reality as being external and prior to ideas or thoughts; contrast the work of the structuralist and post-structuralist thinkers we met earlier. Literary texts are given shape by the writer, and the resulting form may provide a correct or incorrect model of the real. The sort of text providing the best model is found in the nineteenth-century historical novel. Walter Scott's *Waverley* is a novel which, for Lukács, typifies the historical struggles of the two political parties of the late eighteenth century and the Jacobite rebels. The central character, Waverley, is a dreamer, but he is connected to the Tories – an uncle on the land – and to the Whigs – his father in town – and he actually joins the rebels. So he serves the function of ensuring the contact of those 'extremes whose struggle fills the novel, whose clash expresses artistically a great crisis in society'.[25] So Waverley, in spite of his not being average himself, manages to present in the structure of the novel typicality, the joining of the individual and the general in history.

It would be useful to try a Lukácsian approach to *Midnight's Children* as a first move, since the text proclaims precisely the relationship of the individual to history, in this case the birth of India. This text would, however, cause some problems, since it is also alive with 'unmediated totalities', Lukács' phrase for obsessive, minute detail in a text – a kind of ultra-realism. Lukács criticized James Joyce and other modernist writers for their excessive and obsessive detail about individual lives. For example, in Joyce's *Ulysses*, Bloom is found in the kitchen, with the cat:

> He listened to her licking lap. Ham and eggs, no. No good eggs with this drouth. Want pure fresh water. Thursday: not a good day either for mutton kidney at Buckley's. Fried with butter, a shade of pepper. Better a pork kidney at Dlugacz's. While the kettle is boiling.[26]

The presentation of such details grants them a distorted significance, in Lukács' view; they become reality itself, through reification, the process of making human relations reduced to relations between objects. Bloom's humanity is presented as a stream of relations to objects, without any sense of his place in the dialectical struggle of class society.

By way of complete contrast, another Marxist, Theodor Adorno, praises modernist works such as *Ulysses* (see bibliography). He argues that literature does not reflect reality directly, but by a kind of distortion, so that art forms give us a negative knowledge of the world. What we see in Joyce, and in Rushdie for that matter, is the processes of alienation through which the individual is seen as isolated, introverted, self-contemplating, acting with fellow humans only by accident, unaware of the dialectic of history. This, Adorno asserts, is the real state of our condition in the modern world. The implication we draw from reading modernist texts is the possibility of a different state of affairs. Rushdie's text fits Adorno's analysis more fully than

Lukács', but the Lukács analysis is easier to try as a first step. How would either of these theories be used in the classroom? I have instanced the Rushdie because it is a current A Level text. What about D.H. Lawrence's *Sons and Lovers*, Rosa Guy's *The Friends*, Agnes Smedley's *Daughter of Earth*, Alan Sillitoe's *Saturday Night and Sunday Morning*, Barry Hine's *A Kestrel for a Knave*? Any text which deals with the relationships of individuals to social structures may be tackled via Lukács and/or Adorno at some stage, in language which still uses their concepts but not in too complex a form for the pupils – see Paul Moran's article for a series of 'innocent' questions which are conceptually complex.

Both these Marxist thinkers had a fairly straightforward view about language itself, although at times Adorno suggests what might be deconstructive strategies in analysing texts. Pierre Macherey, on the other hand, was a Marxist writer who took on board the structuralists' views on language, and worked new notions about ideology into his *A Theory of Literary Production*. He criticizes traditional criticism for treating the work as a given fact 'to be received, described and assimilated through the procedures of criticism'.[27] For the text is 'generated from the incompatibility of several meanings, the strongest bond by which it is attached to reality in a tense and ever-renewed confrontation.'[28] Not surprisingly, the theorist's task is to show 'a sort of splitting within the work: this division is its unconscious in so far as it possesses one – the unconscious which is history, the play of history beyond its edges, encroaching on those edges; this is why it is possible to trace the path which leads from the haunted work to that which haunts it.'[29] Using these ideas, it is not difficult to see the unconscious of *Women in Love* as World War I. Such a view gives the reader of that novel a chance to comprehend the intense violence which erupts in interpersonal relations through the text.

In order to understand Macherey's approach better, it is important to consider the notion of ideology which figures largely as a frame for his ideas about the text's incompleteness. The topic of ideology is a site of continuing debate among Marxist thinkers. Macherey uses the ideas of Louis Althusser for his own discussions of the role of ideology in textual structure. Marx's own formulations on the concept of ideology may be usefully noted here: 'Consciousness is . . . from the very beginning a social product, and remains so as long as men exist at all.' 'The phantoms of the human brain also are necessary sublimates of men's material life-process.'[30] So the way we live is represented to us and by us as more or less coherent; we have sets of common-sense knowledges which have a practical element built in. Hence we are, according to the concrete circumstances of our lives, rich, poor, women, men, black, white, yellow, and so on. From these material facts there develop out of the system of social and economic relations in a society ways of representing our situation to ourselves. These ways are ideologies; they show how our lives are to be run within a pre-set agenda. Thus: entry condition – 'women are housewives'; function of ideology – how to act as a housewife. The housewife's place is in the home; she makes meals appropriate to dietary fashion; uses technology to save time to be creative and fulfil herself; cares, naturally, for children and husband, oozing goodwill and plenitude; naturally, her desires are satisfied. What more could she want? The picture is of a situation that is natural and universal. It is only 'natural' that women should be cooks and housekeepers while men go off to forage for loadsamoney. In political and educational terms, ideology can be extremely insidious in its workings. To say that X is 'the natural party of government' is an absolute con-trick, but it works. Women are still housewives. So what is a complex process of representation, which is socially produced and therefore variable according to social formations, is made to seem common sense, natural. It is natural to want to raise standards, and it's common sense that we know what they should be.

It should be clear, as Steve Bennison and Jim Porteous show in their article, that ideology cannot deal with contradiction. The heated discussions about the television film *Tumbledown* display this point vividly: the film focused on the Falklands War of 1982, in which Britain fought with Argentina for the possession of the Falkland Islands. It contrasted the suffering of an individual soldier with the public 'triumph' of the military and the implied glory of the British people. In this instance, ideologies of war as a collective act were in clear conflict with ideologies of individual suffering and heroism.

Back to Macherey. He analyses Jules Verne's story *The Mysterious Island*. Verne's small society of castaways are forced to use the natural wealth of their island, but in the course of the story they find that they were not the first colonists. Captain Nemo has been there first! He, Nemo, provides them with a chest of goods. The would-be colonists are thus face-to-face with the signifiers of bourgeois economic relations; they are the 'already written' of the text. Verne, according to Macherey, was attempting to bypass the historical fact of societies necessarily existing before science and technology can be developed. The contemporary ideology of colonialism privileged the positivistic view of science and technology: 'The engineer was to them a microcosm, a compound of every science, a possessor of all human knowledge.'[31] However, as the story develops, the text reveals its fault-lines by acknowledging what had been left out of the beginning – the chest. This strategy brings back the Robinson Crusoe theme that Verne's text had tried to modernize. Robinson Crusoe had the spoils of his society with him before he started work on the island. By permitting, in the production of his text, the theme his ideology wished to exorcize, Verne's story displays precisely the contradictions that the ideology would smooth over.

In general then, texts display contradictions through the working of ideology, through their gaps, through their absent signifiers. What are we to make of the roles for women in the Dickens world, for example? One writer whose texts might well be approached in this way is Samuel Beckett. In her article, Tess Collingborn shows how ideological framing, without the entry into the difficulties of the discourse of ideology, can be used to enable pupils of average and below average ability to make *Endgame* their own. By breaking down the concepts, such as the ideology of, say, womanhood in *Hamlet* through a series of questions – What do the women say? When? To whom? Who listens? Do they make decisions? and so on – it is easily possible to locate ideological patterns, and thus the 'political unconscious'[32] of the text being studied.

Women's voices

The last example enables me to move towards an area of literary theory which has powerful potential to change the practices of English teachers. Feminist theory has taken many forms, but the concept of ideology has been particularly useful in articulating ways in which women are positioned by the economic and social structures of their society. A particularly helpful introduction to this area is to be found in the Open Univeristy's course U221, 'The changing experience of women', units 5 and 6. Once again, it would be invidious, especially for a man, to say that this or that was the origin of feminist theory. Many women writers, however, look back to Virginia Woolf's *A Room of One's Own*. See, for example, Michèle Barrett's essay 'Ideology and the cultural production of gender', at the end of which she concludes: 'It is vital . . . to establish its [gender's] meaning in contemporary capitalism as not simply "difference", but as division, oppression, inequality, internalised inferiority for women. Cultural practice is an essential site of this struggle.'[33] Toril Moi in *Sexual/Textual Politics* (see bibliography) also starts her discourse by referring to different views of women writers on Woolf. Of course, for many pupils reading today, the appeal of Woolf's style may well be limited, and texts such as Smedley's *Daughter of Earth*, Alice Walker's *The Color Purple*, Maya Angelou's *I Know Why The Caged Bird Sings*, or, at another level, Gene Kemp's *The Turbulent Term of Tyke Tyler* would provide easier entry points to the 'woman question' than Woolf.

Moi's book is, in some ways, the clearest introduction to the variety of discourses which have been described as feminist that a reader new to the field of feminist discourse might profit from. She points up the differences between early feminist writers such as Kate Millett and Mary Ellmann and later critics like Elaine Showalter, Sandra Gilbert, and those writing in France such as Hélène Cixous and Julia Kristeva. It is clear to the reader of Moi's text that feminist theorists have covered a wide ground in carving out the terrain of their concerns, and that their approaches are plural, political and urgent. The book is at times not easy to read, unless the reader has had some experience of considering the overall scope and concerns of literary theories from an introductory book by Jefferson and Robey, Eagleton, or Selden. It would also be useful to look at a collection of readings in feminist criticism such as that edited by Mary Eagleton (see bibliography).

Two further references to Virginia Woolf are of interest. Christina Peri Rossi, from Uruguay and living in exile in Spain, is a poet and novelist. In an interview in 1984 she was asked why she thought there were so few women writers in Latin America in comparison with the number of male writers of international reputation. She said 'the Latin American woman is still limited to the domestic and family world with a specific set of duties. As such, she is the victim of circumstances which have prevented her from developing a personal cultural life and a specific space around herself, what Virginia Woolf called a "room of her own".'[34] Personal space and the construction of identity are particularly powerful issues in black women's writing. The contribution in this volume of Gill Murray and Val Fraser reflects the levels of raising consciousness that are required to change entrenched views of this scene: 'their comfortable white view of events'. Margaret Whiteley's article makes it clear that the agenda for studying women's writing, for examining language and oppression by stereotype, is varied and possible within a range of examination work. At one level the important strategy is getting women writers read. On this matter the work of the NATE Language and Gender group must be mentioned. They have raised consciousness among many NATE members about gender issues in English teaching, especially with the publication of *Alice in Genderland,* a varied collection of evidence of sexist practices.[35] Mary Jacobus, in *Reading Woman,* takes up the question of Woolf once more, in a discussion of her notion of androgyny. She uses a deconstructive tactic to revalue Woolf's gesture towards 'the field of signs'. Woolf, in her own writing, suggests the 'difference of view' as rewriting, a 'recognition that all attempts to inscribe female differences within writing are a matter of inscribing women within fictions of one kind or another . . . and . . . that what is at stake for both women writing and writing about women is the rewriting of these fictions . . .'[36] The levels at which this is attempted should be legion.

Bakhtin and Foucault: discourse and power

I have two reasons for leaving until last the work of Mikhail Bakhtin, the Russian writer, and Michel Foucault, the French writer, both of whom were particularly concerned with the relationship between discourse and power. The first is that both writers did not produce a unified body of theory, but rather created a series of related positions on the problems of language, discourse and society. The second is that their ideas can be used as frames for what has been said about other theorists, and thus serves as a reminder that all discourses, including those in this book, are historically situated.

Bakhtin worked in Russia from the early 1920s till the mid-1970s. His own life spanned pre-and post-revolution society. The climate for publishing was of course very oppressive in the Stalinist years, and this may account for the fact that Bakhtin had to publish some of his major works under the names of two of his friends, Voloshinov and Medvedev (see bibliography). His main concerns, to which he returned throughout his life, were language, literature and society. Now, as English teachers, if we are to espouse any common core of interests, we would embrace precisely those theorized by Bakhtin, particularly as he describes language: not a transcendent offering from on high to the deficient, but 'a continuous generative process implemented in the socio-verbal interaction of speakers.'[37] For Bakhtin, writing here under the name of Voloshinov, language is not merely the static system of *langue* (see page 87) but a dynamic, material form of life: 'I give myself verbal shape from another's point of view, ultimately from the point of view of the community to which I belong.'[38] It is instructive to use the Bakhtin theories to comment on the 1988 *Report of The Committee of Inquiry into The Teaching of English Language*, known as the Kingman Report from its chairman, Sir John Kingman, a mathematician.

This report was commissioned by Kenneth Baker, education minister in the ninth year of a new-right Tory government. Its remit included the finding and recommending of a model of English language which would serve as the basis for teacher training and inform professional discussion of all aspects of English teaching. Given the political context of the report it is perhaps not surprising that the languages and dialects of those British citizens whose first language is not standard English are mentioned only in asides. In other words, these manifestations of linguistic diversity are tokenized in the interests of the centripetal (see glossary). This is a term of Bakhtin's which refers to the tendency in any society for one dialect or language to become dominant. In his words:

> Unitary language constitutes the theoretical expression of the historical processes of linguistic unification and centralization, an expression of the centripetal forces of language . . . We are taking language not as a system of abstract grammatical categories, but rather language conceived as ideologically saturated, language as a world view . . . insuring a maximum of mutual understanding in all spheres of ideological life. Thus a unitary language gives expression to forces working towards concrete verbal and ideological unification and centralization, which develop in vital connection with the processes of sociopolitical and cultural centralization.[39]

This point is crucial to understanding the drift of the Kingman Report, which takes standard English to be the only medium for teaching. It reaches this conclusion by a series of sleight-of-hand 'arguments', as for example the notion that 'It is this fact of being the written form which establishes it as the standard. And it is the fact of being the written form which means that it is used not only in Britain but by all writers of English throughout the world, with remarkably little variation' (p. 14). Apart from world English being American in provenance, dialects other than standard are found in written form – *The Canterbury Tales* does exist as words on the page, as does the work of writers such as Linton Kwesi Johnson and John Agard. The Report attempts to elide this kind of inaccuracy by saying blandly that any model of language must be 'to a greater or lesser extent, specific' (p. 15). The soothing disclaimer may be met by Bakhtin's words: '[there is] no word or form left that would be neutral or would belong to no one; all of language turns out to be scattered, permeated with intentions, accented . . . Every word gives off the scent of a profession, a genre, a current, a party, a particular work, a particular man, a generation, an era, a day, and an hour. Every word smells of the context and contexts in which it has lived its intense social life.'[40] The Kingman Report reeks of official oil which cannot smooth over the attempt to centralize the English language as an instrument of power and control.

We can use another concept of Bakhtin's to oppose this kind of strategy, however. Heteroglossia (see glossary) is the tendency in language to be centrifugal, to resist the pressures of the dominant dialect. It literally means 'the tongue of the other', and is a very helpful way of conceptualizing diversity in language. In Bakhtin's words, 'all languages of heteroglossia, whatever the principle underlying them and making them unique, are specific points of view on the world, forms for conceptualizing the world in words, specific world views, each characterized by its own objects, meanings and values . . .'[41] Without such a concept as heteroglossia we are at the mercy of those who would impose upon us their language as the one language, unified, singular, with one voice, transparently reflecting a world without contradictions. Using it we can interrogate the sociopolitical provenance of official pronouncements by analysing their necessary saturation in ideologies. We need to be able to say that it is important for children in our schools to learn through dialects of English other than the standard, and in languages other than English. This is not to do away with the standard; it is to place it as a tool. For many children it does not validate their identity or culture, but alienates. Schools can be alienating enough in their structures. Let us think about the consequences of a centripetal language policy in the context of these words of Bakhtin:

> [the word] exists in other people's mouths, in other people's contexts, serving other people's intentions; it is from there that one must take the word, and make it one's own. And not all words for just anyone submit equally easily to this appropriation, to this seizure and transformation into private property; many words stubbornly resist, others remain alien, sound foreign in the mouth of the one who appropriated them and who now speaks them; they cannot be assimilated into his/her context, and fall out of it; it is as if they put themselves in quotation marks against the will of the speaker. Language is not a neutral medium that passes freely and easily into the private property of the speaker's intentions; it is populated–overpopulated–with the intentions of others.[42]

There is here a powerful recognition of the enormous and critical task of learning language. The place of the individual learner is sensitively demonstrated against the pressure of varieties which themselves carry a form of life. Against this richness the so-called model of Kingman is a thin, authoritarian travesty.

How then should we use Bakhtin in reference to literary texts? Dickens offers many examples of the dialogical principle in action in his novels. Take for instance the celebrated opening of *Hard Times:* 'Now what I want is Facts. Teach these boys and girls nothing but Facts.' This opening piece of centripetal language is dialogized by the heteroglot language of Sissey Jupe. Its authority is undermined by the intractable life of the girl's dialect.

'"Girl number twenty", said Mr Gradgrind . . . "Who is that girl?" "Sissy Jupe, sir, "explained number twenty . . . "Sissy is not a name," said Mr Gradgrind. "Don't call yourself Sissy. Call yourself Cecilia." "It's father as calls me Sissy, sir", . . .'

There is an immediate confrontation between the high dialect and implied culture of Gradgrind and the 'low' dialect of Sissy with its pressure to expression arising from the culture of the circus. As we follow the fortunes of Sissy Jupe and Louisa Gradgrind the conflict is dialogized further by the value placed on the culture of Facts being shown to be emotionally bankrupt. Sissy has strength, although her dialect is heteroglot; better, she is strong because her language is set against the centripetal. We can multiply this instance many times in different novels – *Little Dorrit* is particularly rich and complex in its workings. The final delight of Pancks' verbal assault on Casby is a striking example. The strategy of the Dickens texts also involves the Bakhtinian notion of carnivalization (see glossary). Bakhtin derived this idea from his studies of medieval literature and classical fables, most particularly the work of François Rabelais, in which a systematic opposition to the ideological dominance of the ruling hierarchies was instituted by the celebration of the grossness of the material body. In *Hard Times* the life of Sleary's circus is seen as a 'gross' commentary upon the ordered sterility of Gradgrind's ideology which thereby dialogizes or interrogates it, showing its utter limitations for the life of feeling.

Many writers apart from Dickens may be viewed through Bakhtin's framework of ideas. Angela Carter's *Nights at the Circus* is full of the effects of carnival, from the physical characteristics of the heroine Fevvers, to the feast of fools in book 2, chapter 4, in which the clowns enact a Rabelaisian celebration of the physical. The writer is able to dialogize stereotypes, to interrogate ideology at a number of levels and insert the reader into a maelstrom of activity. Italo Calvino's *If on a winter's night a traveller* is a continuous dialogue with the reader and itself; it draws her in as if it were an innocent text and then laughs at her gullibility. It is a remarkable questioning of the dialogue of writer and reader which also entertains by playing with heteroglossia in the form of different genres. The different 'novels' which the reader is led to believe will develop exhibit the rich variety of the novel as a form. Salman Rushdie's *Midnight's Children* bristles with Bakhtinian effects. The narrator is constantly dialogized in his fantastic stories by the woman he lives with, who brings him down to earth and, in the process, makes the reader aware of the danger of believing a central source. At the end of Book One (p.120), when the hero/narrator is born on the stroke of midnight, as is the state of India, his woman Padma, on his expostulating that his mother was paid only one hundred rupees for his photograph, makes the following dialogical comment: '"Don't be vain", Padma says grumpily, "one hundred rupees is not so little; after all, everybody gets born, it's not such a big big thing."' Later in the novel there is an interesting opposition between the state with its centripetal policy of forcible sterilization of all the children of midnight – the silencing of the creative powers of heteroglossia – and the community of magicians living an alternative life in Delhi, the symbolic home of the new central authority. Rushdie's novel teems with the voices of the other and celebrates in fictional terms the Bakhtinian awareness of myriad life and language in conflict with an oppressive centre. If nothing else, Bakhtin provides the perfect justification for the inclusion in the curriculum of officially marginalized texts; not as tokens, but as living heteroglot opinion on the world.

Complementary to Bakhtin, though perhaps less fruitful, is the French writer Michel Foucault. His main concerns have been with the relationships between discourse and power, and in particular how certain discourses have developed historically. In one of his most concise pieces of writing, 'The Order of Discourse', he shows how conditions and/or qualifications govern admission to certain discourses. He is not only thinking of the initiatory rites of groups such as freemasons, but of the much wider society: '. . . even in the order of "true" discourse, even in the order of discourse that is published and free from all ritual, there are still forms of appropriation of secrets . . . it may well be that the act of writing as it is institutionalized today, in the book, the publishing system and the person of the writer, takes place in a "society of discourse" . . .'[43] In terms of English, the society of discourse has often been a version of cultural nepotism in which the rules have not been disclosed. What texts are on the A Level syllabus? Are Black writers allowed? Is it permissible to study texts by women in a tradition of patriarchal control? Gerald Gregory in *Changing English* [see note 24 to 'English Studies revisited' on page 7] shows clearly how working-class writing has been suppressed or marginalized by the authority of the state. Foucault then points us in the direction of the necessarily social parameters of discourse, and behind the apparent transparency of published discourse to its provenance. He takes us to the relations of power and influence which shore up surface reality. Hence his work is useful for analysing media as well as literary texts, since it moves us below the surface of, say, a news or documentary programme, or of a newspaper leader, to a further network of lines that intersect in the hidden discourses of the powerful.

There is, as Bakhtin said, no first or last dialogue. The words from this section are in your court, to speak about, to dialogize. Of course what is here is only a starter; the bibliography and glossary are the next courses on the menu.

NOTES

1 David Murray, 'Dialogics', in Douglas Tallack, ed., *Literary Theory at Work*, London, Batsford, 1987, p. 128.

2 Ludwig Wittgenstein, *Tractatus Logico-Philosophicus*, London, Routledge and Kegan Paul, 1971, p. 35, cited in Mary Douglas, ed., *Rules and Meanings*, Harmondsworth, Penguin, 1973, p.29.

3 Thomas Hardy, *The Return of the Native*, London, Macmillan, 1968, pp. 11–12.

4 Michael Halliday, 'Linguistic Function and Literary Style: an inquiry into the language of William Golding's *The Inheritors*', part reprinted in Douglas, *Rules and Meanings*, p. 290.

5 William Golding, *The Inheritors*, London, Faber, 1955, pp. 106–7.

6 Douglas, *Rules and Meanings*, p. 288.

7 Roland Barthes, *Mythologies*, trs. Annette Lavers, St. Albans, Paladin, 1973, p. 42.

8 Umberto Eco, *The Role of the Reader*, London, Hutchinson, 1981, p. 146.

9 ibid., p. 154

10 ibid., p. 161

11 ibid., p. 162

12 ibid., p. 163

13 ibid., p. 165

14 ibid., p. 167

15 Jonathan Culler, *Structuralist Poetics*, London, Routledge and Kegan Paul, 1975, p. 137.

16 Raman Selden, *A Reader's Guide to Contempory Literary Theory*, Brighton, Harvester, 1985, p. 73.

17 Roland Barthes, 'The Theory of the Text', in Robert Young, ed., *Untying the Text*, London, Routledge and Kegan Paul, 1981, p. 39.

18 Jane Austen, *Persuasion*, Harmondsworth, Penguin, 1972, p. 237

19 Roland Barthes, *S/Z*, trs. Richard Miller, London, Cape, 1975, p. 12.

20 Elaine Millard, 'Feminism II, Reading as a Woman', in Tallack, *Literary Theory at Work*, pp. 135–57.

21 Paul de Man, 'Semiology and Rhetoric', reprinted in Josue V. Harari, ed., *Textual Strategies*, London, Methuen, 1979, p. 130.

22 Jacques Lacan, *Ecrits*, trs. Alan Sheridan, London, Tavistock, 1977 p. 157.

23 Roman Jakobson and Morris Hallé, *Fundamentals of Language*, The Hague, Mouton, 1956, pp. 69–96.

24 Salman Rushdie, *Midnight's Children*, London, Picador, 1982, p. 26.

25 George Lukács, *The Historical Novel*, Harmondsworth, Penguin, 1969, p.36.

26 James Joyce, *Ulysses*, Harmondsworth, Penguin, 1969, p. 58.

27 Pierre Macherey, *A Theory of Literary Production*, trs. Geoffrey Wall, London, Routledge and Kegan Paul, 1978, p. 13.

28 ibid., p. 80.

29 ibid., p. 94.

30 cf., Valentin Voloshinov, *Marxism and the Philosophy of Language*, trs. Ladislav Matejka and I. R. Titunik, London, Seminar Press, 1973, p. 12.

31 Macherey, *A Theory of Literary Production*, p. 214.

32 Fredric Jameson, *The Political Unconscious: Narrative as a Socially Symbolic Act*, Ithaca, Cornell University Press, 1981.

33 Michèle Barrett, 'Ideology and the cultural production of gender', reprinted in Judith Newton and Deborah Rosenfelt, eds., *Feminist Criticism and Social Change*, London, Methuen, 1985, p. 83.

34 Psiche Hughes, 'Interview with Cristina Peri Rossi', in Mineke Schipper, ed., *Unheard Words*, London, Allison and Busby, 1985, p. 255.

35 *Alice in Genderland*, NATE, 1985.

36 Mary Jacobus, *Reading Woman*, London, Methuen, 1986, p. 40.

37 Voloshinov, *Marxism and the Philosophy of Language*, p. 98.

38 ibid., p. 86.

39 Mikhail Bakhtin, *The Dialogical Imagination*, trs. Caryl Emerson and Michael Holquist, Austin, Texas University Press, 1981, pp. 270–1.

40 ibid., p. 293.

41 ibid., pp. 291–2.

42 ibid., p. 294.

43 Michel Foucault, 'The Order of Discourse', reprinted in Young, *Untying the Text*, p. 62.

Glossary: a harvest of terms

APORIA: a favourite post-structuralist word, this; it means deadlock, the sort of situation one finds oneself in in Tesco's. The richness of meanings, all the fruits of advanced industrial societies, and a few poorer ones force choice; but how can we choose? External criteria prevail and our choice is a compromise, a cop-out. In a text like Yeats's poem 'Among School Children' external criteria, our accepted reading practices, lead us one way. The aporia in the text is its richness, its ability to be read in radically opposed ways; it is a kind of double bind. Here is choice, but you can't make a decision. Look back at Paul Moran's article, and at the de Man essay cited in the bibliography.

AUTHOR: you might think that the author was a painfully obvious term. But, there are various ways of conceptualizing 'the author' according to partic-ular theories. Roland Barthes declared the author 'dead' in an essay in 1968. Richards and Leavis had earlier thought of the author as a supersensitive intelligence who knew more about 'Life' than we do. The New Critics such as Brooks and Wimsatt thought of the author as an organizing intelligence, but as of no more significance than that. They were very similar to the Russian formalists in this respect. For both groups the text itself was the only significant object of study. Derrida acknowledges intentionality by using the concept of presence; he argues that most theories of language use the idea of the speaker's intentions as a full, present force, which the hearer can understand in full likewise. However, Derrida's concept of **différance** defeats all such attempts. See also **logocentric.** Early Marxists such as Lukács considered the author to be a responsible form-giver having a kind of artistic reponsibility to reflect the world accurately. Macherey, by contrast, argues for the author's role to be that of production, the working of raw material into a text. (See theories section). For Bakhtin, the author dialogizes the language of texts, so that they are full of different voices – **heteroglossia.** In structuralist theory the author is of no concern whatever, and neither is the reader, in contrast to Barthes, who celebrates the reader as a powerful figure, the producer of meaning. See also **intention**.

CARNIVALIZATION: one of Bakhtin's notions; it refers to the way dominant forms of literature and language can be undermined by grotesque humour. Angela Carter uses it to great effect in *Nights at the Circus,* in the physical appearance of her heroine Fevvers, and in the circus itself as a metaphor of changed realities. Dickens uses carnival in *Hard Times, Bleak House, Little Dorrit* and *Our Mutual Friend* especially, as a satirical strategy against the forces of oppression. Salman Rushdie finds plenty of scope for carnivalizing India and Pakistan in *Midnight's Children* and *Shame*. Note! Carnival is a much more subversive idea than some liberal humanists (see **liberal humanism**) would like; the best of the Comic Strip films begin to approach its real effect.

CENTRIFUGAL and **CENTRIPETAL:** two terms used by Bakhtin to signal the forces of conflict in *any* language; for example, in the Kingman Report, the model is centripetal, imposing the official view, giving pedagogic language a centre from which to exercise control. The centrifugal is not given much of a voice by Kingman. Dickens is full of the conflict of these tendencies. An extreme example of the dominance of the centripetal is found in Margaret Atwood's *The Handmaid's Tale*.

CLASSIC REALISM: *see* **realism**

CLOSURE: the 'happy ending' is the most stereotyped form of closure in a text. In the classic realist novel of the nineteenth century it takes the form of resolving loose ends, even to the extent of having to disclose the most tortuous of plots, as in *Little Dorrit*. Hardy gives us a nice illustration of the problem of finishing off a text in *The Return of the Native*, where instead of sending the reddleman off into obscurity he has him marry Thomasin, to please his readers. We can see closure at work in the construction of television news programmes – usually reassuring images of the royal family, children, animals or eccentrics occurring at the very end of the bulletin. It is a powerful effect of ideology to make us hanker after stories with neat endings, for this way they make sense. Closure also has a more problematic implication, to do with the distinctions between inner and outer; where am I when I read a text? In the text or in the world? Italo Calvino's novel *If on a winter's night a traveller* is the most entertaining exploration of this problem I know, but you could also read Edward Said (see bibliography).

CODES: this is a generally structuralist way of looking at language and literature; Umberto Eco is the most well-known theorist to use codes in a structuralist approach, though academics would call his work **semiotic.** (See the section on **structuralism** in the theory overview.) Basically a code is a pattern of signification, like traffic lights. Move up a gear, and you can see how language can be thought of usefully as a complex series of codes. But, as you have noticed, Roland Barthes had a rather special version of Code, which Paul Bench's article (q.v.) describes with admirable clarity.

DECONSTRUCTION: any academic would at this point tear up the text and say you cannot be serious. Deconstruction in a few words? And in the form of a definition? But most academics don't face the kind of problems that Paul Moran documents so clearly in his article (q.v.). So some thoughts on deconstruction. It is a word associated with Jacques Derrida especially and, briefly it 'means' meaning is not nice and transparent but full of problems; any interpretation of a text is only a momentary fix of the language and it can always be unfixed. What you do is to read the text of, say, T.S. Eliot's 'The Waste Land' and in the process search for the loose ends or gaps in the text which would let you come back at it and say 'Here is the rupture; this is where the text breaks its own ground rules and can be read differently.' In 'The Waste Land' of course the ground rules of the text seem to be those of fragmented association, from a ragged polyphony of voices. If, however, we home in on the line 'These fragments I have shored against my ruins' and read it literally, the whole project of the poem appears quite different – to make an exclusive cultural code (see Paul Bench's article) which governs the boundaries of identity; putting it rather brutally, it is a case of 'present your fragments and join the club'. See also **discourse** and **power.** Far from being open it appears as a radically closed text. At this point a proper deconstructionist would then show that this second reading is itself subject to further deconstruction; the spectre of **aporia** looms. Fortunately we can use the methods of deconstruction without taking the whole philosophical apparatus on board, as is shown by the articles of Nick Peim and Paul Moran. In strategic terms it is useful to link **deconstruction** with **ideology** and **heteroglossia.**

DEFERRAL (of meaning): a basic post-structuralist principle which recognizes the recursion factor in language, that is, once you start a sentence, you could go on for ever, for example, 'This is the house that . . .'. See Nick Peim's article.

DIFFÉRANCE: this is Jacques Derrida's made-up word which signals the radical instability of meaning; it captures the way words 'strain/Crack and sometimes break, under the burden,/Under the tension, slip, slide, perish,/Decay with imprecision, will not stay in place,/Will not stay still' (T.S. Eliot, *Four Quartets,* 'Burnt Norton' V 149). **Defer** and **differ** are both caught up in **différance.** See Paul Moran's article for its application in the classroom.

DIFFERENCE: the basic principle underlying Saussure's theory of meaning; Cat is not Hat . . . words mean what they do because they don't mean something else. This view abolishes **history** and should be regarded as having limitations.

DIALOGICS: the general term for Bakhtin's theories; see **carnivalization, centrifugal/centripetal, heteroglossia.**

DISCOURSE: the social and historically conditioned practices of groups of human beings using language to articulate views on their worlds; discourses are always **situated,** that is, permeated by **intentions, conceptual frameworks,** and the pressures of **history.** No discourse can be neutral. See Bakhtin and Foucault in the bibliography, and the articles of Nick Peim, Margaret Whiteley, and Gill Murray and Val Fraser.

ENOUNCED and **ENUNCIATION:** two key terms from linguistics; the first refers to the narrated event, that is, the actual words written or spoken; the second refers to the discourse act of the speaker or writer, that is, who, in what circumstances, to whom, enunciates. Joyce has an amusing and satirical version of this distinction in the Ithaca section of *Ulysses*, Penguin 1969 edition, pp. 586–658. See also Tess Collingborn's article; and Easthope in the bibliography.

FEMINISM: lots of ideas at work here; different feminist writers take up different theoretical positions on the world, and on literature; some, for instance Michèle Barrett, use and adapt Marxist frames of reference; French writers such as Hélène Cixous, Luce Irigaray, Julia Kristeva adopt/ adapt ideas from the field of psychoanalysis, especially the writings of Jacques Lacan. Elaine Showalter has, among other focus areas, posited the idea of *gynocriticism*, the concentration on texts written by women including biographical material and letters. One common concern among all feminist writers is to make **gender** an issue for very critical focus, especially by analysing the discourses concerning stereotypes of women and men in literature and society. See the articles mentioned under **discourse**, and Tess Collingborn's remarks on toys in particular. See Toril Moi's book for a sharp introduction to the field. See also the publications of the NATE Language and Gender group.

FORMALISM: usually, Russian; this refers to any theory which concentrates on the formal aspects of a text, such as rhythm, rhyme, metre, plot (or fabula), dominant devices, and so on. It points us in the direction of *patterning* in texts, and is useful at basic levels of raising awareness of structures. The ideas of *foregrounding* and the *dominant* were later developments. See the theories section for more discussion.

GENDER: basically, the construction of behaviour patterns for women and men on the basis of various stereotypes reinforced by dominant ideologies. See Margaret Whiteley's article and that of Gill Murray and Val Fraser. Blatant examples of bias in gender construction abound in the tabloids, in soaps, and much literature presented to us as 'Great'. See **feminism.**

HETEROGLOSSIA: one of Bakhtin's key terms; it refers to the way language is social throughout its life. When anyone uses language it is permeated with the intentions and accents of others. The words I use are always in a state of struggle with their origins outside me, and thus with the institutions which would narrow down language to a **monoglossia,** a single authoritative dialect admitting no variation. In literary theory it is the discourses of the novel as a genre which admit heteroglossia as part of their structural possibility as opposed in general to poetry which tends to allow only the one voice. See the theories section.

HISTORY: for the purposes of this book it is best to describe history as the necessity of any text and any reader/writer being placed at a particular moment in society and within particular circumstances of political and social formations, the significance of which will vary according to the literary theory concerned. Thus for **structuralism** in its pure form, history is not a relevant focus for analysis; a similar story is the case for the New Critics in the USA. For most other theories history is important; in some cases, such as Marxist theories, it is a *sine qua non*.

IDEOLOGY: a hotly contested term, but one which is essential for understanding the ways in which literature and other signifying practices work upon the reader. In simple terms we all have views of reality, everyday practical reality, upon which we base our lives. These views seem natural to us and it is often very difficult to see things differently. Here lies the role of ideology. In particular women have in recent years come up against the power of ideology in trying to reconstruct their lives; what is a housewife, for example? Ideology conceals the fact that housewives are economically significant to the country's overall financial state yet are not recognized for either their work or status value. In literary texts ideology shows itself by gaps and contradictions, especially in the classic realist novel. For example the ideologies through which the society of *Little Dorrit* is transmitted constitute a powerful critique of the oppressive mechanisms which construct the individual. At the same time the very notion of invidualism is criticized by the text's ideology; no one can escape the social formations in which they are made to live, yet awareness of that very necessity, a prerequisite for change, is swept aside by the closure of the novel; Arthur and Amy win, while the 'froward and the vain made their usual uproar'. Some texts deliberately show their play with ideology, such as Salman Rushdie's *Shame*. See the theories section and the article by Steve Bennison and Jim Porteus.

IMAGINARY: Lacan's term for the child's pre-verbal stage of psychic growth; in this stage the child has an illusion of wholeness. When language is learned the rot sets in and the child realizes his or her difference, from parents, and in terms of sex. She then becomes the 'split subject' to whom Tess Collingborn refers in her article. Language sets up the desire to be whole again and the search is often, in literary texts, a painful process. D.H. Lawrence's *The Rainbow* charts these stages of growth in exemplary terms. See also **symbolic**.

INTENTION: a term we all are aware of as a common-sense view of human behaviour, as being forward structured. In literary discourses it refers to the **author** as a person who has intended a certain meaning in a text. This view is held by, for example, Leavis and Richards as clear and straightforward. It is challenged by the Russian formalists and the structuralists who argue that intentions are nothing to do with texts. In this they are joined by the New Critics. For Bakhtin, post-structuralist critics, and Marxist critics, intentions are a focus for conflict and dialogue.

INTERTEXTUALITY: quite a straightforward term. Any text has elements of other texts as its antecedents and refers more or less obliquely to these. In some cases, for example 'The Waste Land,' the references are explicit and purposeful. The idea helps to dispel the sacred notion of originality, so that children can realize that their efforts at writing can borrow from styles and genres without being threatened. (NB Julia Kristeva has a different view of this term; she means something like internal textual relations, the fine webs of the text.)

JOUISSANCE: the pleasure of reading a text of the kind Barthes describes as 'writerly'; in Barthes' terms it is erotic: we can appropriate the notion for the general pleasure of reading without the threat of the One Interpretation. See Paul Bench's article.

LANGUE: Saussure's word for the idealized system of language, the blueprint in the collective brain. Noam Chomsky calls it 'competence'. See also **parole.**

LIBERAL HUMANISM: this term refers to a view of the world, or **ideology,** which centres on the individual as the point of origin of all understanding. It derives from the French philosopher Descartes' well-known fiction 'I think, therefore I am.' If you look at that gnomic saying, you will see it assumes a stable ego from which all else follows; the ego is transcendent and beyond appeal. It is the basis of Leavisite criticism and of many of the practices of teachers of English. One of its least endearing characteristics is that in the appeal to the 'individual' the individual is in fact a blatant stereotype of bourgeois humanity, with appropriate patterns of behaviour and response to literary texts. It ignores the work of Freud and Lacan on the **unconscious** and in fact cannot admit contradiction. See the articles of the contributors *passim*. See also Terry Eagleton and Catherine Belsey in the bibliography.

LOGOCENTRIC: this word is used by Jacques Derrida in particular. He argues that all Western societies' uses of language rely on logos, the Greek for 'word' or 'discourse', or 'principle', and in New Testament Greek, God, as a guarantee of the validity of the particular discourse. It is a kind of ultimate referent; the very last court of appeal, so to speak. Derrida argues, however, that meaning is radically undecidable, and that our fond hopes for certainty are an illusion. See **deconstruction, différance,** Paul Moran's and Nick Peim's articles, and T.S. Eliot's *Four Quartets, passim.*

METACODE or **METALANGUAGE:** a language or, more accurately, register, for discussing or analysing texts, usually in linguistic form, but also in any other cultural signification, such as film, or television, or fashion. See Cathy Twist's article and Roland Barthes' *Mythologies.*

METAPHOR: the figure of language by which one word is substituted for another. Extensions of this basic idea come from Roman Jakobson, who regarded the substitution axis of language as a fundamental organizing principle in literary texts. Metaphor is the dominant organizer of poetry, in Jakobson's scheme. Lacan takes the scope of metaphor a bit further; for him 'metaphor occurs precisely at the point where sense emerges from nonsense'. Metaphor is the controlling figure of the **imaginary,** the illusion of wholeness. See Barbara Johnson in the bibliography.

METONYMY: the figure of language by which a literal reference to one thing or aspect of a thing stands for a whole through its contextual association; 'the poor' have other human attributes than their poverty, but as 'the poor' they are known. Jakobson thought of metonymy as the chaining axis of language; you may recall the way language is described by linguists as working from the intersection of two axes, one of which is that of the chaining or syntagmatic axis. Out of our word stores, or banks, we make choices and link these by rules of syntax to form sentences. But because of the way language is built on differences, sentences are never final and complete. My last sentence could easily have been other. Jakobson applies the metonomy/chaining notion to realist novels in particular. The chaining of events in a complex novel such as *Bleak House* has to be resolved by **closure,** otherwise they could seem indeterminate and thus provide an incomplete world picture for the reader. Lacan developed the idea so as to describe the state of desire, or lack, that our being constructed by the language we inhabit creates. Just as the metonymic axis of language strings out structural possibilities and implies the ever-present possibility of otherness, so in psychoanalytic terms the ego is seen by Lacan as just such a string of positions held under by the Law, or **Phallus.** In somewhat simpler terms, 'I' could always be other, and thus I am always searching for a guaranteed place for my self to rest. In literary texts this has been a dominant focus since *Hamlet.* See Paul Bench's article. See also **symbolic** or **imaginary.**

MONOGLOSSIA: the opposite of **heteroglossia,** language which shuts out all others.

NARRATOLOGY: a grammar of narrative, using **structuralist** notions about language and its coded patterning to try to establish universal principles of constructing stories. See the discussion of Eco on the Bond novels in the theories section and Harold Rosen in the bibliography.

NEW CRITICISM: the work of, in particular, Cleanth Brooks, William Wimsatt and Monroe Beardsley. Their main concern was to concentrate on the text itself, and to regard the variables of **history** and biography as irrelevant; **intention** was also not a legitimate focus for the critic/reader. One of the main effects of the New Critics' position is to imply a community of readers of like-minded sensibilities, for whom the words on the page are made absolutely clear by a process of 'close' reading. See **liberal humanism.** See also the introductory section on English Studies revisited.

PAROLE: Saussure's term for individual utterances, which use the rules of **langue.** Chomsky terms this 'performance'. See the theories section on **structuralism.**

PATRIARCHY: the rule of the father, and therefore, by metonymy, of men in general. Feminist theorists use the term extensively in their analyses of both literature and power. See the theories section on **feminism,** and the articles by Margaret Whiteley and Gill Murray and Val Fraser.

PHALLUS: not quite what it appears to be. Jacques Lacan argued, in re-writing Freud, that children learn language and sexual identity at the same stage; gender differentiation is controlled by patriarchal laws which make incest taboo, and desire for parents is repressed into the uncon-scious by the Law, which has an all-powerful symbol, the Phallus. Thus the Phallus is an empty signifier – empty since it does not signify any organ – which conditions language and desire. In the entry into language the child is made to realize his or her difference as a being who is not whole (see **imaginary** and **symbolic)** and thus subject to the desire for wholeness. Since language is always of the Other – that is outside and anterior to the child – the child's desire is for the Other and its privileged signifier, the Phallus. So, putting that more simply, it is a sort of absolute rule-maker and an absolutely desired object; no one has one, but everyone wants one. Lacan appears to be documenting an unfairly loaded power structure of pressures on identity which feminist writers have called phallocentric. The final signifier is derived from the male organ and thus creates the dis-courses of male domination, or phallogocentrism! There is some argument about this area; the general issues are discussed in Toril Moi's book; see the bibliography.

PHENOMENOLOGY: the name given to very diverse writings by, for instance, Husserl, Heidegger, Sartre. See Eagleton, *Literary Theory*, chapter 2, and Nick Peim's article.

POLYPHONY: many voices in a text; the literary expression of **heteroglossia;** examples abound in Dickens' *Little Dorrit*, Joyce's *Ulysses*, Rushdie's *Midnight's Children*. But be careful; polyphony is not just a cosy debate which is resolved by the author, but an expression of conflicting voices and ideologies. On these grounds, only the Rushdie text really qualifies as polyphonic, since it leaves the reader uncertain as to where to locate 'truth'. Bakhtin's exemplar of polyphony was Dostoevsky.

POST-STRUCTURALISM: a blanket term for a whole variety of theories which broke with the rigid patterning of the structuralists. See the theories section and bibliography. See also Cathy Twist's and Nick Peim's articles. In a nutshell, the term involves showing texts as plural, having many meanings according to the way they are read, a final meaning is unde-cidable, and undesirable.

PSYCHOANALYTIC CRITICISM: a very wide-ranging term which covers a number of writers and positions; an excellent summary of the field is found in Terry Eagleton's *Literary Theory*, chapter 5. See bibliography.

READER-RESPONSE CRITICISM: again an umbrella term; for a group of theories which try to locate all the action of reading in the reader; the most well-known exponents of this area are German and American. See the bibliography and Paul Bench's article.

REALISM: a concept that has many forms; theorists such as Colin MacCabe have devised the category of **classic realism** to analyse the predominant forms of fiction and cinema; its features include the setting up of an enigma, or puzzle, its resolution, the hierarchizing of discourses, and a final closure through which the text is well rounded off. Classic realism can include such works as *Middlemarch* and such popular fictions as those of Agatha Christie. What classic realism cannot handle is contradiction; even if there are individual moral dilemmas, these are ascribed to character. See bibliography.

REPERTOIRE: a term associated with Wolfgang Iser, who divided the reader into an 'implied' and 'actual' reader; the first of these is the reader whom the text creates for itself, the second is the actual reader whose historical experience encodes a repertoire of responses to texts. See Paul Bench and Paul Moran for further discussion.

SEMIOTICS or **SEMIOLOGY:** the sciences of signs.

SIGN: in Saussure's linguistics the sign consisted of two parts, the signifier, or sound image, and the signified, or concept. It is based therefore on a binary system of relationships. The sign had meaning through difference, and was an arbitrary construction, but the relationship between its parts, once established, was stable, a structure. Signs have other forms; they can be Iconic, that is with a resemblance between the two parts as in a portrait and its sitter; Indexical, with a causal relationship between the two parts – a sign with smoke on it to warn of fire risk, and Signs Proper, in which the relationship is a matter of social convention, as in language. See bibliography and the articles of Paul Bench and Nick Peim.

SIGNIFIER and **SIGNIFIED:** see **SIGN.**

STRUCTURALISM: using Saussure's linguistics as a basis, various theorists have developed analytic ways of examining texts which regard the texts as signifying systems consisting of self-sufficient and self-bounded structures of interlocking relationships, built on the principle of binary opposition, or difference (see **sign**). See the theories section, particularly the examples from Eco, and the bibliography. Any form of cultural practice can be analysed through a structuralist framework – cinema, advertising, television, fashion, cars . . .

SYMBOLIC (THE): the other term in Lacan's awful equation of the two opposed states of the psyche. It's the mode of existence our poor ego finds itself in when we have learned language, and are therefore subject to desire, since language allows us no fixed resting place, no 'still centre'. Most of Western literature since *Hamlet* seems in some measure at least to exhibit this restless search for finality. D.H. Lawrence's *Women in Love* is a good example; even the apparently conventional keeps the search going with Birkin's final words, 'I don't believe that.' See Paul Bench's opening paragraph. See also **imaginary** and **phallus.**

TRACE: this is Derrida's term for the way a text appears to have a meaning which is definite and determined; he is referring to the meanings of the text which are not there and which constitute the differences from the current text. Any text therefore has its trace as a basis of its very existence. A useful link can be made with this concept and **ideology.**

UNCONSCIOUS: in Freudian writings, the dynamic sub-system of the mind which is part of a larger system of conflicting forces. In literary theory its application is to what the text conceals, omits, elides. See Nick Peim's article, and Fredric Jameson, *The Political Unconscious,* in the bibliography.

Bibliography

The books cited are asterisked for relative difficulty. One * denotes first year university student level; two ** indicates second/third year level; three *** denotes challenging texts which should not be read without preparation at a lower level. The books are in subject blocks, and follow the order of the theories in the theories section. At the beginning I have cited some introductory texts which should lead you on from this volume and serve as bridge texts for the more detailed works in each section.

Introductory texts

Lodge, David, *Modern Criticism and Theory, A Reader*. London, Longman, 1988 *

Eagleton, Terry, *Literary Theory: An Introduction*. Oxford, Blackwell, 1983 *
  A lively read, politically aligned, sceptical and informative.

Jefferson, Ann, and David Robey (eds.), *Modern Literary Theory: A Comparative Introduction* (second edition). London, Batsford, 1986 *
  Generally clear and informative, if slightly dense and dry at times.

Selden, Raman, *A Reader's Guide to Contemporary Literary Theory*. Brighton, Harvester, 1985 *
  Very clear and straightforward, but slightly short on detail.

Tallack, Douglas, (ed.), *Literary Theory at Work*. London, Batsford, 1987 *(*)
  An excellent collection of applications of theories to three literary texts; detailed and at times difficult, but always interesting.

Russian formalism

Bennett, Tony, *Formalism and Marxism*. London, Methuen, 1979 **
  More specialized, but very interesting discussion of key issues. Lively and readable.

Matejka, Ladislav, and Krystyna Pomorska, *Readings in Russian Poetics: Formalist and Structuralist Views*. London, MIT Press, 1971 **
  Lots of the original work of the formalists; not particularly difficult to read, but with some very Russian concerns, as on metrics, sometimes making the going harder.

Linguistics and structuralism

The key text is:

de Saussure, Ferdinand, *Course in General Linguistics,* trs. William Baskin. London, Fontana/Collins, 1974 **
  Essential reading – quite readable and clear; difficult only at times in points of detail. Try it!

Barthes, Roland, *Mythologies,* trs. Annette Lavers. St Albans, Granada Publishing Ltd., 1973 *
  Lively, wide-ranging use of structuralist ideas to analyse all kinds of cultural signification. A similar application of the conceptual framework Barthes uses has been carried out on popular television programmes in: Masterman, Len, (ed.), *Television Mythologies.* London, Comedia, 1984.

Culler, Jonathan, *Structuralist Poetics: Structuralism, Linguistics and the Study of Literature.* London, Routledge and Kegan Paul, 1975 **
  A clear survey of the whole field; see Paul Bench's article.

Eco, Umberto, *The Role of the Reader: Explorations in the Semiotics of Texts.* London, Hutchinson, 1981 **
  Very variable in difficulty, but the essay on the Bond novels is riveting. See the theories section.

Genette, Gerard, *Figures of Literary Discourse,* trs. Alan Sheridan. Oxford, Blackwell, 1982 **
  See especially chapter 7, 'Frontiers of Narrative' – an excellent summary of the problems of narration.

Genette, Gerard, *Narrative Discourse,* trs. Jane E. Lewin. Oxford, Blackwell, 1982 **
  Complex and detailed at times, with a fascinating analysis of Proust, but accessible after reading Harold Rosen (q.v.).

Greimas, A.J., *Semantique structurale.* Paris, Larousse, 1966 **
  See Paul Bench's article, Roland Barthes' *Image–Music–Text* and Fredric Jameson's *The Political Unconscious.*

Halliday, Michael, *Explorations in the Functions of Language.* London, Edward Arnold, 1973 *
  A varied collection of articles on language from a sociolinguistic point of view, including the analysis of William Golding's *The Inheritors* referred to in the theories section.

Hawkes, Terence, *Structuralism and Semiotics.* London, Methuen, 1977 *
  Very clear and comprehensive introduction to a wide range of issues across the field of theory – occasionally **.

Jameson, Fredric, *The Prison-House of Language: A Critical Account of Structuralism and Russian Formalism.* Princeton University Press, 1972 **(*)

Brilliant but sometimes tough analysis of the limitations of linguistic and structural analysis as the author sees it.

Lodge, David, *The Modes of Modern Writing: Metaphor, Metonymy and the Typology of Modern Literature*. London, Edward Arnold, 1977 *
Readable and interesting exploration of these key concepts in analysing change in literary form.

Rosen, Harold, *Stories and Meanings*. NATE, 1985 *
Excellent short introduction to recent theoretical work on narrative.

Post-structuralism

Barthes, Roland, *Image–Music–Text*, trs. Stephen Heath. London, Fontana, 1977 *
See especially 'The Death of the Author', a short, provocative key text which undoes many assumptions about the authority of the 'author', and leads the way to reader power.

Barthes, Roland, *S/Z*, trs. Richard Miller. London, Cape, 1975 **
An engrossing *tour de force;* Barthes reads a short novel by Balzac, *Sarrasine,* through a grid of reading units (lexias) and codes. See Paul Bench's article for a clear exposition of the codes, and Elaine Millard in *Literary Theory at Work* (q.v.) pp. 135–57, for an analysis of D.H. Lawrence's *St Mawr* through a feminist appropriation of the codes.

Belsey, Catherine, *Critical Practice*. London, Methuen, 1980 *
A very crisp and incisive analysis of the differences between older theories such as New Criticism and post-structuralist work. Some good textual readings, e.g. of a Conan Doyle story, from a deconstructive view.

Blonsky, Marshall, (ed.), *On Signs*. Oxford, Blackwell, 1985 **
A very varied and interesting collection of mainly post-structuralist writings, including work on television and photographs.

Culler, Jonathan, *On Deconstruction: Theory and Criticism after Structuralism*. London, Routledge and Kegan Paul, 1983 **
Very elegant and readable – an interesting section on 'reading as a woman'. Possibly a bit smooth for its subject's abrasions.

Derrida, Jacques, *Of Grammatology*, trs. Gayatri Chakravorty Spivak. London, Johns Hopkins University Press, 1976 ***
Some accessible material, particularly the sections on Rousseau. The introduction of the translator is useful. *But* it is very hard, except in small doses. See Paul Moran's article.

Harari, Josue V., (ed.), *Textual Strategies: Perspectives in Post-structuralist Criticism*. Ithaca, Cornell University Press, 1979 **(*)
Some very useful essays, especially from the editor, 'Critical Factions/

Critical Fictions'; Paul de Man, 'Semiology and Rhetoric'; Jacques Derrida, 'The Logic of the Supplement'; Edward Said, 'The Text, the World, the Critic'. All the contributions are challenging!

Johnson, Barbara, *The Critical Difference: Essays in the Contemporary Rhetoric of Reading*. London, Johns Hopkins University Press, 1980 **
Very elegant and acute yet witty deconstructive readings of texts; an interesting discussion of metaphor/metonymy in Baudelaire's 'L' Invitation au Voyage', and a brilliant deconstruction of Derrida deconstructing Lacan deconstructing Poe; do try this – it's a kind of limit(less) text for the deconstructive strategy.

Leitch, Vincent B., *Deconstructive Criticism: An Advanced Introduction*. London, Hutchinson, 1983 **
Traces the philosophical roots of deconstruction – sometimes in a playful and deconstructive way, generally engaging the reader in a challenging dialogue.

Ryan, Michael, *Marxism and Deconstruction: A Critical Articulation*. London, Johns Hopkins University Press, 1982 **
A brilliant, if at times problematical, confrontation of two key bodies of theory. Worth the effort.

Said, Edward W., *The World, the Text and the Critic*. London, Faber, 1983 **
A wide-ranging collection of essays which use a variety of insights from Post-structuralism, Marxism and Foucault.

Williamson, Judith, *Decoding Advertisements*. London, Marion Boyars, 1984 **
Very fascinating analysis of advertisements, using Lacan especially; there is a clear account of the imaginary and the symbolic.

Young, Robert, (ed.), *Untying the Text*. London, Routledge and Kegan Paul, 1981 **
Some very important essays; from Roland Barthes, Etienne Balibar and Pierre Macherey, Michel Foucault in particular, plus two by Barbara Johnson from *The Critical Difference* (q.v.).

Marxism

Selden, Raman, *A Reader's Guide to Contemporary Literary Theory*, includes a very clear and concise guide to the scope of Marxist literary theories in chapter two; see bibliography, introductory texts. *

Adorno, Theodor W., *Prisms*. London, Neville Spearman, 1967 **
A key text of the Frankfurt School – art as negative knowledge, see the theories section – with essays on Huxley, jazz, Walter Benjamin (a highly individual Marxist critic) and other topics.

Benjamin, Walter, *Illuminations*, ed. Hannah Arendt. New York, Harcourt Brace Jovanovich, 1968 **
Some key essays, including 'The Work of Art in the Age of Mechanical Reproduction'. See also Terry Eagleton, bibliography.

Dowling, William C., *Jameson, Althusser, Marx: An Introduction to The Political Unconscious*. London, Methuen, 1984 **
A really useful introduction to many issues in contemporary Marxist theory using the focus of Jameson (q.v.).

Eagleton, Terry, *Criticism and Ideology*. London, New Left Books, 1976 **
A very interesting text which involves an attempt to establish a scientific materialist criticism – see also Feminism, Michèle Barrett.

Eagleton, Terry, *Walter Benjamin, or Towards a Revolutionary Criticism*. London, New Left Books, 1981 **
A radical change of direction, with a focus on a much more political criticism; see the last words of Paul Moran's article.

Jameson, Fredric, *Marxism and Form*. Princeton University Press, 1971 **
A powerful, complex analysis of main twentieth century Marxist theorists.

Jameson, Fredric, *The Political Unconscious: Narrative as a Socially Symbolic Act*. Ithaca, Cornell University Press, 1981 **(*)
A powerful and complex book, which engages the post-structuralist enclosure of the text with the social and cultural heterogeneity of history. Read Dowling (q.v.) first.

Lukács, Georg, *The Historical Novel*. London, Merlin Press, 1962 **
A classic text, establishing the 'reflection model' of literature – see the theories section.

Lukács, Georg, *The Meaning of Contemporary Realism*. London, Merlin Press, 1962 **
A fascinating attack on writers such as Joyce, Beckett, Proust and Kafka for their use of minute detail and concentration on the individual.

Macherey, Pierre, *A Theory of Literary Production*, trs. Geoffrey Wall. London, Routledge and Kegan Paul, 1978 **
Uneven but very interesting; his ideas can be applied to prose and poetry with equal ease.

Voloshinov, Valentin, (Mikhail Bakhtin), *Marxism and the Philosophy of Language*, trs. Ladislav Matejka and I. R. Titunik. London, Seminar Press, 1973 **
A very important text, almost certainly written by Bakhtin, which lays the ground for a materialist philosophy of language, and provides a clear conceptualization of the necessarily social functions of language. See also Harold Rosen, bibliography.

Feminism

Moi, Toril, *Sexual/Textual Politics*. London, Methuen, 1985 *(*)
   This is still the best overall introduction to the field, with strong argumen-
   tation and great clarity of style. At times prior knowledge of more basic
   theories is required.

de Beauvoir, Simone, *The Second Sex*, trs. H.M. Parshley. Harmondsworth,
   Penguin, 1974 **
   Classic groundwork in the field.

Coates, Jennifer, *Women, Men and Language*. London, Longman, 1986 *
   See Margaret Whiteley's article.

Eagleton, Mary, (ed.), *Feminist Literary Theory: A Reader*. Oxford, Blackwell,
   1986 **
   A very useful collection of articles and essays; see references in Margaret
   Whiteley's article.

Ellmann, Mary, *Thinking about Women*. London, Virago, 1979 **
   A brilliant, ironic debunk of 'phallic' criticism.

Gallop, Jane, *Feminism and Psychoanalysis: The Daughter's Seduction*. London,
   Macmillan, 1982 **
   A confrontation with Lacan's 'phallocentrism'.

Gilbert, Sandra M., and Susan Gubar, *The Madwoman in the Attic: The Woman
   Writer and the Nineteenth-Century Literary Imagination*. New Haven, Yale
   University Press, 1979 **
   A huge undertaking, inevitably flawed; suggestive and challenging.

Jacobus, Mary, *Reading Women: Essays in Feminist Criticism*. London,
   Methuen, 1986 **(*)
   Some complex and elegant essays, owing much to deconstruction for their
   technique; very interesting on Virginia Woolf.

Kristeva, Julia, *The Julia Kristeva Reader*, ed. Toril Moi. Oxford, Blackwell,
   1985 **(*)
   Of considerable importance, but Kristeva is a very difficult writer at times;
   read Moi's introductions first.

Millet, Kate, *Sexual Politics*. London, Virago, 1977 **
   Classic examination of patriarchal attitudes in fiction, but regarded as too
   straightforwardly polemical today.

Milroy, Lesley, 'Social Network and Language Maintenance', in Barbara
   Mayor and A.K. Pugh, (eds.), *Language, Communication and Education*.
   London, Croom Helm, 1987, pp. 78–84 *
   See Margaret Whiteley's article.

Moers, Ellen, *Literary Women*. London, The Women's Press, 1977 *
   Pioneering, but now shows its cracks. See Margaret Whiteley's article.

Newton, Judith, and Deborah Rosenfelt, (eds.), *Feminist Criticism and Social Change*. London, Methuen, 1985 **
A hard-hitting collection of materialist essays including Michèle Barrett on the cultural production of gender.

Showalter, Elaine, *A Literature of Their Own: British Women Novelists from Brontë to Lessing*. London, Virago, 1978 **
Wide-ranging and scholarly, but with some theoretical problems; see Toril Moi, Introduction to *Sexual/Textual Politics*.

Woolf, Virginia, *A Room of One's Own*. London, Granada Publishing Ltd., 1977 **
A very important text which has provoked a wide variety of reactions from women writers; see Toril Moi, ibid.

Bakhtin and Foucault: discourse and power

Bakhtin, Mikhail, *The Dialogic Imagination*, trs. Caryl Emerson and Michael Holquist. Austin, Texas University Press, 1981 **
Indispensable for getting into Bakhtin's ideas on dialogics, especially the essay 'Discourse in the Novel'.

Bakhtin, Mikhail, *Problems of Dostoevsky's Poetics*, trs. Caryl Emerson. Manchester University Press, 1984 **
Much more specialized, but full of challenging ideas.

Bakhtin, Mikhail, *Rabelais and his World*, trs. Helen Iswolsky. MIT Press, 1968 **
The initial focus may seem far removed, but it's a text with much to offer to the twentieth-century reader/teacher; the notion of carnivalization receives a full treatment.

Clark, Katerina, and Michael Holquist, *Mikhail Bakhtin*. Harvard University Press, 1984 **
A rich source of Russian intellectual background material and a clear exposition of Bakhtin's ideas.

Foucault, Michel, *The Foucault Reader*, ed. Paul Rabinow. Harmondsworth, Penguin, 1986 **
A basic anthology of key Foucault writings on the relationships between discourses and power.

Foucault, Michel, *The Archaeology of Knowledge*, trs. A.M. Sheridan Smith. London, Tavistock, 1972 **
A general discussion of the principles underlying his earlier studies on madness and medicine.

Medvedev, P.N., *The Formal Method in Literary Scholarship*, trs. A.J. Wehrle. London, Johns Hopkins University Press, 1973 **

A detailed interrogation of formalism and an attempt to make a synthesis of inner and outer (written, at least in large part, by Bakhtin).

Todorov, Tzvetan, *Mikhail Bakhtin: The Dialogical Principle*, trs. Wlad Godzich. Manchester University Press, 1984 **
An excellent overview of all the Bakhtin writings, giving a clear expression to his philosophical position.

Voloshinov, Valentin, *Freudianism: A Marxist Critique*, trs. I.R. Titunik. New York, Academic Press, 1973 **
A powerful confrontation of individualistic theories of subjectivity (almost certainly written by Bakhtin). See also the entry for Voloshinov under Marxism.

Reader-oriented theories

Fish, Stanley, *Is There a Text in This Class?* Harvard University Press, 1980 **
Key essays by one of the most well-known theorists in this area, including 'Literature in the Reader' referred to by Paul Bench.

Holland, Norman, *Five Readers Reading*. London, Yale University Press, 1975 **
A view of the reading process from a psychological framework. Interesting and provocative. See Paul Bench's article.

Holub, Robert C., (ed.), *Reception Theory: A Critical Introduction*. London, Methuen, 1984 **
A useful introduction to the German branch of reader theories.

Iser, Wolfgang, *The Act of Reading: A Theory of Aesthetic Response*. London, Johns Hopkins University Press, 1978 **
A classic statement of a particular view of the reader; see Paul Bench's article.

Index